Lift Me Up

He sets on
high those who are
lowly, and those who mourn
are lifted to safety.
—Job 5:11

Alice Cravens Moore

Publishing Designs, Inc.
Huntsville, Alabama

Publishing Designs, Inc.
P.O. Box 3241
Huntsville, Alabama 35810

Cover images: iStock.com

Book design and layout: Crosslin Creative.net

Editors: Debra G. Wright, Peggy Coulter

Printed in the United States of America

Publisher's Cataloging-in-Publication Data

Alice Cravens Moore 1947—

Lift Me Up/ Alice Cravens Moore

144 pp.

13 chapters and study questions

1. Awareness of God's Power. 2. Safety in Trust 3. Discipline for Daily Christian Living

I. Title.

ISBN 978-1-945127-16-8

248.8

Dedication

To the Tuesday morning ladies' class
at North Jackson Church of Christ
in Jackson, Tennessee, but
especially to Phyllis, my friend
of many years

Acknowledgments

Much gratitude is due to Peggy Cole Coulter and Debra G. Wright. May God bless both of them as they, too, strive to be lifted up.

Other Books
by
Alice Cravens Moore

A New Song

Ways Which Be in Christ

Comforted of God

Finding Hannah

Queenie and the Back Porch Swing

Contents

Introduction: Lift Me Up 9

1 Do Not Consent 13

2 Know the Power of Your Hand 25

3 Keep Your Heart 37

4 Understand the Fear of the Lord 45

5 Be One Who Wins Souls 57

6 Speak a Good Word 67

7 Acknowledge the Eyes of the Lord 77

8 Practice Being Merry 87

9 Pray the Prayer of the Upright 99

10 Accept That Safety Is of the Lord 109

11 Be Responsible When Fueling Fires 117

12 Dole Out the Honey 125

13 Seek to Be Well-Advised 133

Addendum 141

Sources Cited 143

Introduction
Lift Me Up

"The fear of man brings a snare:
but whoever trusts in the Lord
shall be safe." Proverbs 29:25

The Lord lifts up those who trust in Him, those who believe to the point of obedience and glorify His name by walking in the light. God truly lifts up His children as they overcome sin and make their way toward heaven. The apostle Paul wrote, "And the Lord will deliver me from every evil work and preserve me for His heavenly kingdom" (2 Timothy 4:18).

Do I really believe those words Paul wrote to Timothy? Do I trust, as did Paul, that God is at work in my life to aid me and help me in my passage through this world?

I certainly am not as strong as Paul. I am sometimes frightened by many things, but that is part of the human condition. And the uncertainty is intensified if God is not the center of one's existence. Obedience to the gospel, an ever-growing faith in God, an intense involvement in Scripture, an acknowledgment of the great sacrifice that Jesus made, and the realization that the Father has a plan for our lives provide an antidote for fear. I need to remember Paul's words to the church in Rome, "If God is for us, who can be against us?" (Romans 8:31).

Are you afraid of being alone because you've lost those dear to you? Are you scared because you have no one on whom to depend when problems arise? Are you apprehensive about growing older and perhaps becoming frail or ill, or are you young and unattached and anxious about what the future holds? Are you troubled about how to bring up your children, or are you worried that your adult offspring are disobedient or not living up to their potential in God's kingdom, the church? Are you fearful because of the possibility of financial problems? Are you afraid of death? The list is endless.

I have been prey to many worries and misgivings and have felt dread and apprehension all too often in my life. Yet, when I give in to these fears and anxieties and allow them to take hold in my mind and in my life, I must realize that I am allowing Satan—how politically incorrect it is to believe in the existence of the devil!—to have power over me. God is always in control, and He takes care of His own. Henry F. Lyte, in his beautiful hymn, "Abide with Me," called God the "Help of the helpless." In my own experience, my Lord has never refused to aid me. My God has never failed to make a way for me, and there is no reason to think that He will stop helping me now. The primary lesson I have had to learn is that God's way is not always my way (Isaiah 55:8–9).

In times of doubt, in times of fear, I simply have to remember that God is keeping watch, waiting and willing to lift me up. One only has to recognize God's power and grace as the psalmist did when he petitioned the Father, "Hold me up, and I shall be safe" (Psalm 119:117). I need also to acknowledge in my heart as did the psalmist, "The Lord raises those who are bowed down; the Lord loves the righteous" (Psalm 146:8).

There's an adage that states, "Give your problems to God—He's up all night anyway." Once again it was an unnamed psalmist who said, "He who keeps you will not slumber" (Psalm 121:3). I realize that it is the nation of Israel that was spoken of in this scripture, but the principle applies to any child of God. Our Lord neither slumbers nor sleeps. In the intensive-care waiting room of life, the Father is keeping vigil with us and for us.

Solomon, the writer of most of Proverbs, expressed the thought that God wants to lift us up another way. "The name of the Lord is a strong tower; the righteous run to it, and are safe" (Proverbs 18:10). Remember that the phrase "is safe" is a Hebrew expression that really means "is set aloft." The idea is that one is secure—one is lifted up—when he is in proper relationship with God.

> *Hold me up,*
> *and I shall*
> *be safe.*
> **—Psalm 119:117**

Even though God's chosen people, the children of Israel, deviated from God's plan for them over and over again, in reality, they knew only the Lord could help them or lift them up. Each time the Hebrew people turned to Him, they realized God was the source of relief for their problems, whether those problems were physical or spiritual, and He was the one who could raise them up above their difficulties. The prophet Isaiah communicated that idea even more succinctly when he wrote, "For I, the Lord your God, will hold your right hand, saying to you, 'Fear not, I will help you'" (Isaiah 41:13).

Oh, yes, I want God to help me and hold my right hand, and my left one also, for that matter, especially when the going gets rough. Life is so much easier when one asks God to hold her up and help her stand.

The chapters in this book include an examination of thirteen scriptures from the book of Proverbs that can serve as a reminder that the Lord our God fully intends to lift us up if we will only allow Him to do so. Oh, I want Him to set me on high and claim me for His own. Don't you?

1

Do Not Consent

"My son, if sinners entice you, do
not consent." Proverbs 1:10

When an individual is tempted to behave in such a way she knows is wrong, she does not have to sin; she still has the power to choose the right course. One does not have to succumb to temptation. There is always a way out. Solomon advised that we always act on that option of refusal. It was Solomon, the third king of Israel, not some twentieth-century slogan writer, who first said, "Just say no." Solomon cautioned, "My son, if sinners entice you, do not consent" (Proverbs 1:10).

Inspired by the Spirit, the apostle Paul put it another way,

No temptation has overtaken you except such as is common to man; but God is faithful, who will not allow you to be tempted beyond what you are able, but with the temptation will also make the way of escape, that you may be able to bear it (1 Corinthians 10:13).

Resisting sin is a continuous process, day in and day out. Admittedly, it is not always easy, but it can be done. Of course, there are ways that we can protect ourselves up front. There are things that we can do to prevent temptation from entering our lives unnecessarily.

Choose Your Friends Wisely

We can choose our friends carefully. We can determine to surround ourselves with those who will help us get to heaven rather than hinder our progress toward that magnificent place. Do your friends exert a negative or positive influence on your spiritual life? Make no mistake; it will be one or the other. Neutrality in friendship is not possible. Someone once said that friendship is not a spectator sport. We are involved with our friends either to our benefit or our detriment. As a teenager, I chose many friends who did not help me in my Christian walk, and even today, I still thank God that He allowed me to live through that period in my life until I learned to choose my friends more wisely. Many of us, if we are truthful, could probably make that statement.

Sometimes the power of the devil comes in the guise of a friend whom we dearly love. If the influence exerted on us by our companions or family is negative or harmful in some way, it is a certainty that Satan has his hand in the relationship and that he is pleased at the results. The devil may even make us feel secure in the company of those who may be detrimental to our spiritual health. Our reasoning may become clouded.

As my children were growing up, they would sometimes blame a friend for their own inappropriate behavior by saying, "He asked me to do it." I would respond with that age-old mother's-reply, "If he asked you to jump off a cliff, would you do that also?" Then I would quote Exodus 23:2, "You shall not follow a crowd to do evil."

We may allow those we love to cause us to lose control. Yet it is the individual's responsibility to govern his own behavior. From the beginning, humans have been prone to blame others. Adam blamed Eve for his sin: "The woman whom You gave to be with me, she gave me of the tree, and I ate" (Genesis 3:12). Yet on the day of judgment, each of us will face God and give an account of our lives. We will not be able to point the finger of blame at someone else. Each of us is answerable for her actions. It will not be acceptable to say, "My friend caused me to drink or do drugs or to gossip or to be unkind or to steal or to lie or to sin sexually."

⤳ You Alone Are Responsible

Paul wrote to the church in Rome, "So then each of us shall give account of himself to God" (Romans 14:12). That same apostle worded the warning somewhat differently in a letter to the Christians in Corinth. "For we must all appear before the judgment seat of Christ, that each one may receive the things done in the body, according to what he has done, whether good or bad" (2 Corinthians 5:10). Those are sobering thoughts. God is going to hold me responsible for my behavior, and He will judge me accordingly. The friends I have chosen will certainly have been an influence on my sentence or acquittal and my punishment or reward, but I alone am responsible. If there is blame to bear, it will be mine.

Joseph realized the importance of "Do not consent." Do you remember that Potiphar, one of Pharaoh's officers, had "left all that he had in Joseph's hand" (Genesis 39:6)? It would have been so easy for Joseph to take advantage of his position.

However, Joseph was a man of God as well as an honest servant.

Imagine how emotionally torn Joseph must have felt when Potiphar's wife asked him to have sexual intercourse with her, not once but "day by day" (Genesis 39:10). Mrs. Potiphar nagged Joseph and assaulted him daily with requests to fulfill her illicit desires. Without a doubt, Joseph was a young virile man, and it would have been so easy to say, "What difference will it make? No one will know."

So then each of us shall give account of himself to God.

—Romans 14:12

Yet Joseph did not consent to forbidden sex. He did not give in to the enticement of that woman. He did not agree to an adulterous relationship. In fact, he told her, "How then can I do this great wickedness, and sin against God?" (Genesis 39:9). We tend to forget that every sin is against God. Other lives may be affected by our sins, but ultimately, it is God who is wronged. David knew that (Psalm 51:4).

A person may suffer for doing right. Joseph did, and many times we will also, at least temporarily. Still God did not desert Joseph. We are told, "The Lord was with him; and whatever he did, the Lord made it to prosper" (Genesis 39:23). Paul warned Timothy, "Yes, and all who desire to live godly in Christ Jesus will suffer persecution" (2 Timothy 3:12).

Because truly living righteously will bring suffering, I have grown to value greatly the words that Paul wrote to Timothy, "This is a faithful saying: For if we died with Him, we shall also live with Him. If we endure, we shall also reign with Him" (2 Timothy 2:11–12). Isn't that a wonderful thought! We will reign with Jesus! That sounds a whole lot like being set on high.

When we allow God to lift us up, we will consistently follow God's plan for our lives and will flourish in every way that matters. Oh, we may not have great wealth or power or fame, but we will possess that which is priceless—a relationship with the Father based on our belief in Him and our obedience to Him. We can be joyful because the peace of God which surpasses all understanding is ours for the taking when we refuse to be anxious, when we're prayerful, when we're thankful (Philippians 4:4–7).

Don't Trade Eternity for a Moment

As Joseph looked beyond his circumstances, he realized that his life had followed a pattern designed by God. His jealous brothers meant evil against him, but God used all that had happened for Joseph's good (Genesis 50:20). In doing what was right, refusing to yield to sin for a season, Joseph saved not only his life but also the lives of all his father's house.

It is vitally important for Christians today to look for God's design in their lives rather than giving in to what seems right for the moment, by associating with companions who will corrupt, or by becoming a partaker of worldly pleasures that can lead to spiritual atrophy or even a complete falling away from Christ.

Solomon wrote, "Can a man take fire to his bosom, and his clothes not be burned?" (Proverbs 6:27). We tend to become like those with whom we associate. Even the world knows this. The lyrics of the country song, "Play with Fire," proclaim:

"Don't be concerned. It's time I learned. Those who play with fire get burned."

⮞ Are You Different?

Because it was undoubtedly an important concept, Paul wrote on two different occasions that "a little leaven leavens the whole lump" (1 Corinthians 5:6; Galatians 5:9). Why should a child of God want to blend in with the world and become one of them? A Christian should stand apart. A Christian should be different. We are to be "special" people (1 Peter 2:9), and if we aren't special, if we aren't different from the world, it is very likely that we are not walking in the light (1 John 1:6–7).

In a long intercessory prayer, the Messiah Himself stressed that while His disciples are in the world, they should not be of the world. Jesus entreated the Father for protection from Satan for His followers. "I do not pray that You should take them out of the world, but that You should keep them from the evil one" (John 17:15). How wonderful and reassuring that the Son of God was not only praying for His apostles and other first-century disciples, but He was also imploring God on behalf of those of us who follow Him today. The Savior of the world prayed for me; He prayed for you. "I do not pray for these alone, but also for those who will believe in Me through their word" (John 17:20).

Yes, it is important to remember Paul's warning concerning the company we keep. "Do not be deceived, 'Evil company corrupts good habits'" (1 Corinthians 15:33). If we are not careful, the influence of worldly associates can lead us to spiritual destruction. What seems to be clever sophistication is actually a highly contagious spiritual disease. Rather than blooming and flourishing religiously, we may wither and our beliefs may die if we allow ourselves to be infected by poorly chosen friends. People of similar personalities or interests tend to associate with one another. Birds of a feather really do flock together. As Christians we need to be striving to imitate Jesus rather than aping people who possess suspect morals and engage in un-righteous behavior. We need to interact with those individu-als who encourage us to live godly lives rather than with those who would corrupt us. Without a doubt, we will become like those with whom we congregate.

Paul phrased this same idea another way when he com-municated with the church at Ephesus: "And have no fellow-ship with the unfruitful works of darkness, but rather expose them" (Ephesians 5:11).

Just as a mirror reflects one's countenance, the hearts of compan-ions mimic each other's thoughts, plans, and actions. "As in water face reflects face, so a man's heart re-veals the man" (Proverbs 27:19). One modern paraphrase (*The Book*) states that verse another way, "A mirror reflects a man's face, but what he is really like is shown by the friends he chooses."

> The Messiah Himself stressed they should not be of the world.

It is only common sense to have as friends those who will help us to grow spiritually and emotionally. "He who walks with wise men will be wise, but the companion of fools will be de-stroyed" (Proverbs 13:20). On two different occasions I have seen young mothers divorce husbands and destroy families simply because a best friend had just done the same thing. These were Christian women who chose their friends poorly. As a result lives were destroyed, or at the very least, negatively changed forever.

In the World, Be a Light

However, we do not need to be fanatical in our avoidance of certain individuals. If we become sufficient unto ourselves or isolated from others, how do we reach out to the lost? After all, we are *in* the world, just not *of* the world. To avoid any contact that might be harmful, we would have to stay locked up somewhere in a room all alone. People who say they do not go to church because some church-goers are hypocrites are not thinking very logically. Here is an unsigned article in a church bulletin that expressed that thought well.

> The man who says he is kept away from religion by hypocrites is not influenced by them anywhere else. Business is full of them, but if he sees a chance at making money, he does not stop for that. Society is crowded with them, and yet he never thinks of becoming a hermit. Married life is full of them, but that doesn't make him remain a bachelor. Hell is full of them, and yet he doesn't do a thing to keep himself from going there. He wants to have you think that he is trying to avoid the society of hypocrites, and yet he takes not a single step toward heaven, the only place no hypocrites can go!

Rather than being influenced adversely by questionable companions, we need to be strong enough spiritually and emotionally to have a positive effect on them when our paths cross.

Paul wrote to the Christians in Rome, "For none of us lives to himself, and no one dies to himself" (Romans 14:7). We can influence others for the cause of Christ by the lives we live daily.

⋙ A Smooth Path

An easy way to avoid giving in to sin is to keep our lives simple. One of the most beautiful requests in the Bible was made by David, the shepherd and king, who petitioned, "Teach me Your way, O Lord, and lead me in a smooth path, because of my enemies" (Psalm 27:11). We should remember that those who would entice us to sin are our enemies, even if they wear the guise of friends. If our friends are urging us to possess more, spend more, or even rush more, for all practical purposes, they may have become our enemies.

The psalmist's prayer was both simple and profound: "Lead me in a smooth path, God." Perhaps David's request should be ours. It is much easier for God to lift us up when we are not concerned about the trappings of the world.

✦ *Lead me in a smooth path, God.* Let me walk around hate rather than through it. Even before the destruction of September 11, 2001, it was obvious that there was much hate in the world, but I don't have to let that hate complicate my life or touch me unnecessarily. Make me aware that hatred is a breeding ground for sin.

✦ *Lead me in a smooth path, God.* Help me to walk without fear or needless worry and doubt. Help me to recognize problems that I can't solve and march on to other things. Yet at the same time, let me walk with the fear that is a true concern and which leads to knowledge, and to change that will help me to consent not to sin.

✝ *Lead me in a smooth path, God.* Help me to keep confusion from underfoot. Keep me lifted up. Remind me that with focused effort, I can lead a calm orderly existence, at least as far as my spiritual life is concerned.

✝ *Lead me in a smooth path, God.* Walk in front of me as I make decisions. Help me to avoid poor judgments and senseless mistakes. Help me to make right any wrongs that I have done to others. In fact, Lord, help me to recognize when I have caused others pain.

✝ *Lead me in a smooth path, God.* If I come to places where there is no road, help me to build one with hope rather than with despair.

✝ *Lead me in a smooth path, God.* Don't allow my life to get too complex, but keep me busy. Keep me working. Let any recreation be filled with innocent activities. Help me to purge any appearance of evil from my life (1 Thessalonians 5:22). Let mischief be left far behind. If social media or any form of technology is distracting me from a close walk with You, cause me to put those things aside. Remind me of the psalmist's words, "Turn away my eyes from looking at worthless things, and revive me in Your way" (Psalm 119:37).

✝ *Lead me in a smooth path, God,* as I refuse to consent to do evil. Let that path be so smooth and plain that I can see any obstacles and, with Your help, overcome them. Remind me, Lord, who I am and where I am going. When I am enticed, and I will be at some point in time, help me not to consent. Lift me up, Lord. Keep me safe.

Questions

1. What advice does Solomon give to a person who is tempted to sin? (Read Proverbs 1:10.)

2. How can one protect herself from temptation? Why is it important to choose friends carefully?

3. What disguise might the devil wear?

4. Is each individual responsible for her own actions? How do you know this? (Read Romans 14:12 and 2 Corinthians 5:10.)

5. How did Joseph avoid being enticed by sin?

6. Explain Proverbs 6:27.

7. What application does 1 Corinthians 15:33 have in our lives?

8. Can one isolate herself from sin totally? Explain your answer.

9. What does Romans 14:7 tell us about personal responsibility to others?

10. What did David mean when he asked God to lead him in "a smooth path"?

My Progress

What have you learned about enticement?

2

Know the Power Of Your Hand

"Do not withhold good from those to whom it is due, when it is in the power of your hand to do so" (Proverbs 3:27).

If God is to lift us up, we must love others, and the proof of that love is our service to them. Sometimes others do not want us to love them, or at least they behave as if they don't. In those cases, service may become difficult or even hindered. The actions of others, however, do not relieve us from our responsibility to them.

Johnny Ramsey, a minister of the gospel, once told a story about a boy and his dog. It seems that the young man and animal were the very best of friends. They did everything together, and because there was such a deep bond between boy and dog, they were practically inseparable. One day the dog was caught in a wire fence and could not free himself. When his master attempted to release the dog's hind legs, the animal bit him. Instinct had kicked in, and the dog was doing only what came naturally. Still, the boy did not retaliate or leave his friend. Instead, he worked from another position to free his dog. The young man loved his pet enough to keep trying to serve him.

We need to love others to such a degree that even when they behave in an unlovable manner, we won't give up on them—at least, not until we have done everything possible to help them. Matthew 10:12–14 depicts a scenario where it may not be possible to love or aid people as we would wish. Yes, it is true that there may come a time when a person has to "shake off the dust under your feet as a testimony against them" (Mark 6:11), but often we accept defeat much too soon. Perhaps we may have to employ a different strategy, just as the little boy did to help his dog. It is almost always in the power of our hands to help others, and God will lift us up for doing so.

The Power in Your Hand

Sometimes it is such a little thing. I live on a busy highway, so I was not surprised when a stranger rang my doorbell one Sunday afternoon. He told me that he had delivered pizza to our house before. Then he said his father was in the hospital, and he needed money for gas in order to take his mother to visit. He asked for ten dollars and promised to pay it back the following Friday. The man was neat and mannerly, and I thought what a blow to his pride it must have been to ask a stranger for money. I only had nine dollars, but I gave it to him as a gift—not as a loan—and I assure you the blessing was mine more than it was his.

Oh, I am not so naive that I don't realize that his story may not have been true, but the blessing was still mine because my

26

soul was warmed by the encounter. Not only that, but God knows my heart as well as the heart of the man who came to the door. It was in the power of my hand to help, so I did.

Nehemiah, cupbearer to King Artaxerxes of Persia, used the power that was in his hand to return to Judah in order to rebuild the broken-down walls of Jerusalem. Along with those who labored with him, Nehemiah knew the potential that lay within their grasp. Facing opposition from Samaritans, Ammonites, Philistines, and Arabs, Nehemiah rallied God's people, and the walls were rebuilt in fifty-two days (Nehemiah 6:15). Scripture records the method with which they persevered, "Those who built on the wall, and those who carried burdens, loaded themselves so that with one hand they worked at construction, and with the other held a weapon" (Nehemiah 4:17).

That particular project involved mental preparation as well as physical exertion. The progress of the repair of the wall around Jerusalem was hindered by many enemies and scoffers. The Lord's people, however, "had a mind to work" (Nehemiah 4:6). They used the power within their hands to help themselves to overcome and to serve. As a result, the Lord lifted them up.

➤ Pay It Forward

Service should be a pattern in our lives that is repeated again and again. Each one of us has been helped by the power of others' hands somewhere along the line. Here is an anonymous quote that phrases that thought well:

> If you are successful, remember that somewhere, some-time, someone gave you a lift or an idea that started you in

the right direction. Remember also that you are indebted to life until you help some less fortunate person just as you were helped.

I truly believe those words. Modern philosophers call it "paying it forward."

My personal debt to others is great because so many individuals have contributed to make me who I am today. I cannot begin to tell you how poor my family was when I was a child. There was very little money for food and other essentials, much less any extras. In those days, no government aid was available, and there were no other avenues of relief. We either made do, or we did without. My father was a proud man who worked hard and did the best he could with what he had.

> My shoes were falling apart.

The day my mother died I had worn her shoes to school because my shoes were literally falling apart. My mother and I put crumpled paper in the toes of her flats so they would stay on my feet. When the school bus brought me back to my house that afternoon, my mother was in great physical distress. I will never forget arriving home and seeing her sitting in the porch swing. Her lips were blue due to lack of oxygen, and that image was indelibly burned into my memory. I returned my mother's shoes to her, and they were still on her feet when she died on the way to the hospital.

Yet many people noticed my family's hardships and wanted to help. I graduated from college only because three of my former schoolteachers, who had watched as I grew up and knew my circumstances, came to my house and told me, "You will continue your education." They arranged for a scholarship, paid for my books the first semester, and put me in touch with others who could help me along the way. The only method that I could ever use to show my gratitude to Miss Zula, Miss Georgia, and Miss Beth was to help my own students during the thirty years I taught school. I tried to instill in them just how much we owe to one another. Those three wonderful women departed this life many years ago, but they share something in common with Abel in that being dead (Hebrews 11:4), they still speak because of the good they did to me and the influence they had on my life and, through me, countless others.

Hold on to God's Hand

I treasure the prophetic writings of Isaiah, who by inspiration penned some of the most beautiful advice concerning the use of the power within us. He wrote, "Strengthen the weak hands, and make firm the feeble knees. Say to those who are fearful-hearted, 'Be strong; do not fear!'" (Isaiah 35:3–4).

The same prophet also advised, "Fear not, for I am with you; be not dismayed, for I am your God. I will strengthen you, yes, I will help you, I will uphold you with My righteous right hand" (Isaiah 41:10). There it is again—that recurring metaphor of the Lord our God, holding us up with His hand or, in other words, lifting us up.

Jesus said that His sheep would never be pulled from His hand.

My sheep hear My voice, and I know them, and they follow Me. And I give them eternal life; and they shall never perish; neither shall anyone snatch them out of My hand. My Father, who has given them to Me, is greater than all; and no one is able to snatch them out of My Father's hand (John 10:27–29).

As long as we do not release the hand of Jesus, He will hold on to us.

The only way we can lose the strength, the joy, the hope that God's hand offers is to let go of His hand. When we hold on to God's hand, we are enabled to use the power which lies within our own reach. When we do our part, God allows nothing to separate us from His love. If you doubt that, just read Romans 8:38–39.

For I am persuaded that neither death nor life, nor angels nor principalities nor powers, nor things present nor things to come, nor height nor depth, nor any other created thing, shall be able to separate us from the love of God which is in Christ Jesus our Lord.

Hands That Do Good

Inspired by the Holy Spirit, the apostle Paul commands us to use the power of our hands to serve one another.

And let us not grow weary while doing good, for in due season we shall reap, if we do not lose heart. Therefore, as we have opportunity, let us do good to all, especially to those who are of the household of faith (Galatians 6:9–10).

Another inspired writer put it this way, "But do not forget to do good and to share, for with such sacrifices God is well pleased" (Hebrews 13:16).

We must use the power of our hands in the here and now. Why wait until some tomorrow that may or may not come? As opportunities arise for service to others, we must seize them. On all too many occasions, I have missed the chance to help others because I acted too slowly or did not recognize the opportunity. Am I so busy or so selfishly occupied with my own daily concerns that I am ignoring the pleas and cries of those around me? I can think of at least two instances when my intentions were good, but I did not follow through and death intervened.

✦ Make that hospital visit.

✦ Call someone who is lonely.

✦ Take that small token to the nursing home.

✦ Send that card or write that note.

✦ Be charitable at every possible occasion.

Regret is truly an unpalatable dish. In addition, when we use the power of our hands for good, we are the ones who receive a greater blessing (Acts 20:35).

It is also in the power of our hands to do good to ourselves—to be happy, to lead productive lives, and to ultimately bring glory to God by our influence. I once heard a profound statement made by Peter Maurin: "The future will be different if we make the present different." That is a thought worth considering. In other words, the conduct of my todays will determine the status of my tomorrows.

What I Want, What I Need

However, it is important that we set appropriate goals and understand what is truly of value as we utilize the power within our hands. All too often we sit at the altar of our possessions and allow material things to become idols in our lives. It is not uncommon for Christians to adhere to a gospel of prosperity, expecting God to give them what they want rather than what they need. That is one of Satan's lies.

What I want might not be to my benefit, either physically or spiritually. When I consider Paul's message to the church of Philippi, I am assured that the Father will give me all I need—not all I desire. "And my God shall supply all your need according to His riches in glory by Christ Jesus" (Philippians 4:19).

True happiness comes from helping others as we walk in the light, not from the accumulations of worldly goods. Many appear to be waiting for some future time when suddenly they will possess more friends, a great family, a new car, a bigger house, or more money. These folks have convinced themselves that instant happiness would be theirs if only that day would come when they somehow obtained those longed-for assets. Then, when they are content, they will have the time, the money, and the talents to help others. That time never arrives.

Some people believe that if only they were wealthy, they would be happy and therefore helpful to others. Yet how many times have you read of individuals winning the lottery or a sweepstakes, and within a short time, those folks have realized that money cannot bring contentment? Wealth, especially sudden financial prosperity, can bring its own type of peril and unhappiness.

Others seek fame as a road to happiness and contentment, but the roster of celebrities whose lives have been shortened because they could not handle their renown and the trappings that went with it is long indeed. Think of the many superstars or pop idols who have succumbed to drug overdoses or preventable accidents. The blatant promiscuity which often is a part of the lifestyle of household names also carries with it broken marriages and neglected or unhappy children who only repeat the cycle. The fame of most of these people was not used to help others or even themselves, and the notoriety was a debit rather than an asset.

Live in the Present

If by chance, something we want, or think we want, falls into our laps, it will not, in and of itself, make us happy. If a person is not happy in the present, the odds are that she will not be in the future either, no matter what occurs. If she is not using the power within her hands now to be of service, it is doubtful that a change in circumstances would alter her behavior.

Life is not a matter of waiting for something to happen, because life simply does not work that way. We have to exert ourselves to make things happen. Contentment does not come simply by waiting long enough. Happiness comes by doing, by accomplishing, by working. It is found along the way to a goal, rather than by the realization of that goal, and those aims should be ones of which God would approve. In His sermon on the mount, Jesus gave specific guidelines for being blessed or, in modern terminology, happy (Matthew 5:3–11).

In order to be happy, we must live in the here and now and deal with life's challenges in a way that pleases God. If we do that, we will be equipped to deal with whatever the future brings. A modern-day philosopher, Rollo May, put this idea another way when he said, "The most effective way to ensure the value of the future is to confront the present courageously and constructively." The apostle Paul phrased it even more adequately when he wrote to the church at Ephesus, "See then that you walk circumspectly, not as fools, but as wise, redeeming the time, because the days are evil" (Ephesians 5:15–16). I want to redeem the time because God will lift me up when I do so.

> God is Lord of the present tense.

If we are going to find a treasure or live a great adventure or contribute to our world, we need to be doing it today instead of some hazy tomorrow. We need to employ the power within our hands now. Each day should be so valuable to us that we do not throw it away or waste the happiness of even one minute of it by trying to live in the future. We cheat ourselves and those around us if we are so unhappy with today that we must constantly think of next week or next year. I pray daily that God will help me to redeem the time.

Even though the Father has both the past and the future in His hand, one should remember that our God is Lord of the present tense. His name is I AM (Exodus 3:14). James understood that concept when he wrote, "Whereas you do not know what will happen tomorrow. For what is your life? It is a vapor, that appears for a little time, and then vanishes away" (James 4:14). We must live in the present, for that is all we have.

The only true happiness comes from knowing that one is in a covenant relationship with God. Striving to walk in the light brings joy, contentment, and peace. In my own life, learning to want what I already have and being thankful for those blessings has brought great delight. Because my happiness is based on God's plan, I can live in the present, not in the past, and not in some uncertain future. I love the words of the prophet Isaiah, "I will greatly rejoice in the Lord. My soul shall be joyful in my God; for He has clothed me with the garments of salvation, He has covered me with the robe of righteousness" (Isaiah 61:10). It is in the power of my hand to take enjoyment and wonder from each hour that the Father chooses to give me, and it is in my power now to aid others.

The Lord lifts us up when we choose to live in the present, using the power within our hands to serve Him and our fellow man. Our faith in Jesus Christ, the blessed Son of God, can sustain us as we use that power from day to day. The incredible Fanny J. Crosby expressed that thought so beautifully in the second verse of her lovely hymn, "A Wonderful Savior." She wrote,

> A wonderful Savior is Jesus my Lord,
> He taketh my burden away;
> He holdeth me up, and I shall not be moved,
> He giveth me strength as my day.

Lasting happiness is achieved when Jesus is Lord of our lives. Yes, it is through Jesus that we are held up, and it is through belief in Him and our obedience to the gospel He gave to us that will cause God the Father to lift us up.

— Questions —

1. What is the proof of our love to others? Explain.

2. Discuss situations when people might not allow us to love them. How might that negate our responsibility in light of Matthew 10:12–14?

3. Discuss times when others have served you or helped you, perhaps even loved you, when you were unlovable.

4. How did Nehemiah use the power within his hand? Was Nehemiah a man of action? Explain.

5. What does it mean when God says that He will uphold us with His righteous right hand (Isaiah 41:10)?

6. Explain Galatians 6:9–10. How should we fulfill specific obligations to others?

7. How is happiness found? Apply the guidelines given in Matthew 5:3–11.

8. Why should we live in the present? (Read James 4:14.)

— My Progress —

What have you learned about doing good?

3

Keep Your Heart

"Keep your heart with all diligence, for out
of it spring the issues of life." Proverbs 4:23

To maintain diligence means to be constant in effort. Diligence involves undivided attention. Solomon instructed us to keep our hearts with continuous effort, with unwavering mindfulness. Through wisdom given to him by God, Solomon realized that the human heart is casually changeable and inconstant by nature. We must stand guard over our hearts if we are to maintain any sort of control over our lives. The effects and consequences that govern our day-to-day existence have their source in the human heart and proceed from there to influence our lives for good or bad.

It can be so easy to denounce others for not keeping their hearts "with all diligence" when they stray into sin. However, unless we have been tested by the same temptation and know whereof we speak, we need to be careful in passing judgment. It takes little effort on our part to condemn when we really don't know what we are talking about—when we actually can't comprehend the trial that another has faced. It is true that we might overcome sin in the same situation, but then again, we might not. A Native American adage says, "Do not judge your neighbor until you walk two moons in his moccasins."

This fact was brought home time and time again to me after the death of my first husband, Bob, many years ago. Being a single parent is never easy regardless of how that state came to be. Things that I thought would never present a problem or even give me a fleeting moment of anxiety actually caused me to stumble, and I had to turn to God again and again for help, for forgiveness, and for strength when I failed.

A hefty dose of self-realization caused me to understand that I have been guilty of a "holier than thou" attitude on more than one occasion. To have learned that I am not as strong or as much in control as I had thought has brought both fear and humility to my existence. Yet, this acknowledgment of my lack of self-sufficiency has taught me to be more patient with the failings of others. I have become more forgiving and less judgmental, pausing to remove the plank from my eye before I attempt to remove the speck from another's eye (Matthew 7:1–4). One of my favorite scriptures is James 2:13, "For judgment is without mercy to the one who has shown no mercy. Mercy triumphs over judgment." I must extend the same mercy to others that God has shown toward me.

Be Aware of Vulnerabilities

Everyone has an Achilles' heel, a physical or spiritual weakness. Even Paul had "a thorn in the flesh" (2 Corinthians 12:7). We may just not have identified it yet, but under certain conditions, that weakness can take charge and overwhelm us if we are not truly attempting to keep our hearts. I have known ministers of God's Word who I thought would never stray or give in to Satan's false promises, but sadly, they did.

The apostle Peter who assured our Savior that he would be with Him to the point of death is a case in point (Matthew 26:35). Yet Peter denied our Lord three times (Matthew 26:69–75). In fact, all the apostles deserted Him on that terrible night of betrayal. If those men who walked daily with Jesus during His time on earth needed to be made stronger, I most certainly will need to be strengthened. Becoming aware of one's vulnerabilities is the first step toward overcoming those weaknesses. With God's help we can keep our hearts, and the Father will continue to lift us up.

Ask God for Another Heart

Do you remember reading about the time that Samuel anointed Saul to be the first king over Israel? Saul was told that he would "be turned into another man." As a matter of fact, "God gave him another heart" (1 Samuel 10:6–9). If the hearts we have prove to be too unreliable or too fickle to maintain our spirituality, perhaps we should pray to God and ask Him for another heart. We need to be willing to do whatever is necessary to get our lives in order and to keep them that way.

I need to ask God for another heart . . .

+ When I feel the need to criticize rather than looking for something to praise.

+ When I am depressed or feeling sorry for myself and cannot recognize all the areas in my life for which I should be happy. In my selfish whining, I am ignoring all the good things

God furnishes me each day. I once heard a thirty-second thought for the day on local television, and the speaker's message has remained with me. He said when we have trauma, heartache, or trials in our lives that we should focus on what is left rather than what is lost. I need to ask God daily to help me to both remember and count my blessings.

✦ When I am busy regretting the past, fretting about the present, and entertaining fears about the future. I should remember that Jesus Christ is "the same yesterday, and today, and forever" and determine to lean on Him for strength (Hebrews 13:8). John the revelator put that thought another way when he wrote, "Grace to you and peace from Him who is and who was and who is to come" (Revelation 1:4). An Old Testament prophet knew this truth as well when he spoke God's words, "For I am the Lord, I do not change" (Malachi 3:6).

Where Is Your Heart?

We need to keep in mind the words of God's servant Paul who advised, "And do not be conformed to this world, but be transformed by the renewing of your mind, that you may prove what is that good and acceptable and perfect will of God" (Romans 12:2). The word *mind* in this verse is the Greek word *nous*. It refers to the intellect. We truly have to change our cognitive faculties and our thought processes as well as our hearts in order to achieve this transformation that Paul writes about, and we can do that with God's help.

The psalmist wrote, "My flesh and my heart fail; but God is the strength of my heart and my portion forever" (Psalm 73:26).

The word *strength* in that verse means *rock*. Is God the rock of my heart? Is He the firm spot in my life where I can feel safe?

Perhaps we have trouble keeping our hearts with all diligence because we don't know where our hearts are, or maybe we have left our hearts in the wrong place. Jesus said, "For where your treasure is, there your heart will be also" (Matthew 6:21). If our hearts are in the world, we are going to have great difficulty in the area of spiritual diligence.

I know a woman, a Christian, who has since chosen the world over Christ. "God wants me to be happy" rather than "what would God have me to do" is her mindset now. Broken families and damaged lives have been the result.

> Maybe we have left our hearts in the wrong place.

Paul wrote, "Set your mind on things above, not on things on the earth" (Colossians 3:2). We can't be near to God and He can't lift us up when our hearts are far from Him.

Several years ago, I heard a story about an older couple who had gone for a ride in the country. In the course of the afternoon, they saw a young couple, also out for a drive, who were sitting almost on top of one another. The older woman said, "I remember when we used to sit that close while out in the car." Her husband, sitting behind the steering wheel, answered, "Well, I'm not the one who moved." If we feel that we are not as close to God as we would like, we should take note that God is not the one who moved.

The Pharisees considered themselves to be a group especially close to God. They were highly religious and supposedly well taught in the ways of God, yet Jesus told them of a prophecy by Isaiah that was fulfilled in them. "These people draw near to Me with their mouth, and honor Me with their lips, but their heart is far from Me" (Matthew 15:8). We need to be careful that we as children of God are not guilty of that same attitude. We should remember as did the psalmist, "It is good for me to draw near to God" (Psalm 73:28), but we must draw near to Him in all ways—with our intellect, our emotions, and our actions.

Watch Your Feet

> Put away from you a deceitful mouth, and put perverse lips far from you. Let your eyes look straight ahead, and your eyelids look right before you. Ponder the path of your feet, and let all your ways be established. Do not turn to the right or the left; remove your foot from evil (Proverbs 4:24–27).

The independent clause, "let all your ways be established," reminds us that we need to be careful of the turnings that we take in life. When we ponder the path of our feet, which is just a metaphorical expression for keeping our hearts with all diligence, we will follow the right way.

Very possibly, when you were in middle school or high school, you read William Golding's classic, *Lord of the Flies*. In that novel, Ralph, one of the primary characters, came to a realization while walking on the beach.

> Ralph chose the firm strip as a path because he needed to think, and only here could he allow his feet to move without

having to watch them. Suddenly, pacing by the water, he was overcome with astonishment. He found himself understanding the wearisomeness of this life, where every path was an improvisation and a considerable part of one's waking life was spent watching one's feet (Golding 76).

David realized that fact when he prayed for guidance and support. "Cause me to hear Your lovingkindness in the morning, for in You do I trust; cause me to know the way in which I should walk, for I lift up my soul to You" (Psalm 143:8).

As we walk through this world watching our feet, we have to make certain that we know where we are going as well as where we have been. That isn't so difficult with God's help. In spite of what the character Ralph thought in the novel, there is no such thing as a "firm strip" where we do not have to watch where our feet are taking us. When we stop watching, Satan will lead us off the path in a hurry. Once again, it was an inspired psalmist who wrote, "Oh, bless our God, you peoples! And make the voice of His praise to be heard, who keeps our soul among the living, and does not allow our feet to be moved" (Psalm 66:8–9).

The prophet Jeremiah knew that it was to God to whom we must look also. "Give glory to the Lord your God, before He causes darkness, and before your feet stumble on the dark mountains, and while you are looking for light, He turns it into the shadow of death, and makes it dense darkness" (Jeremiah 13:16).

Still again, it was a psalmist who described the happy state of the godly, of those who are attempting to keep their hearts with all diligence, of those who are watching their feet.

Because he has set his love upon Me, therefore will I deliver him; I will set him on high, because he has known My name. He shall call upon Me, and I will answer him; I will be with him in trouble; I will deliver him and honor him. With long life I will satisfy him, and show him My salvation (Psalm 91:14–16).

Questions

1. What does *diligence* mean in terms of keeping our hearts? (See Proverbs 4:23.)

2. Why do we need to be very careful before condemning others? Have you ever been guilty of being "holier than thou"? If so, how did you correct your actions?

3. Are there areas where each of us might be weak spiritually? How do we identify these weaknesses? How do we protect ourselves from them?

4. Why should we sometimes pray for "another heart"?

5. Does Jesus ever change? How do you know? (Read Hebrews 13:8; Revelation 1:4; and Malachi 3:6.)

6. Where should our hearts be? List some scriptures that prove your answer.

7. Explain the extended metaphor of watching one's feet.

8. Why will God set you on high? (Read Psalm 91:14–16.) How will God show this elevation?

My Progress

What have you learned about the human heart?

4

Understand The Fear of the Lord

"The fear of the Lord prolongs days,
but the years of the wicked will be
shortened." Proverbs 10:27

The word *prolongs* in our text for this chapter really means *adds*. The fear of the Lord adds days to our lives. This thought is developed more than once in the pages of God's Word, and a beautiful theme throughout Scripture is that God longs to bless His people. Try doing a word study of *bless*, *blessed*, or *blessings*. The idea that God seeks to bless His children is evident throughout the Bible.

Two types of fear are discussed in Scripture. One is negative; one is positive. One is from Satan; one is from God.

Negative Fear

There is the fear that comes from Satan which brings torment and apprehension about what might happen in our lives. This type of fear is sinful and negative, and it does not come from God. Another of my favorite scriptures reminds me to beware of the type of fear that cripples, "For God has not given us a spirit of fear, but of power and of love and of a sound mind (2 Timothy 1:7).

The wrong kind of fear encourages us to be anxious and overly concerned about the future. I dealt with that kind of fear when my young husband Bob died of leukemia. How could God possibly lift me up if I remained filled with fear and mistrust? As I dealt with my grief, I had to renew my trust in God and learn to lean on Him. I wrote a poem not long after Bob's death that helped me to crystallize my attitude.

For Bob Who Went on Ahead

I met with Fear along the way,
He tried to take my hand.
I shrugged him off and pushed him down
And ran and ran and ran.

Despair slipped up from behind
And touched me on the shoulder.
"Oh, no you don't," said Trust in God;
I will not let you hold her.

"Remove this cup," I begged and cried.
"I can't drink it any longer."
"Oh, yes, you can," said Strength from God;
"In the end, you will be stronger."

Thus I continue along the way,
There is much for me to learn.

> Both Trust and Strength still walk with me,
> And God's at every turn.

Inappropriate fear causes us to shrink back from God, and that fear offers no peace—only dread of sorrow, desolation, or punishment. This worldly fear fills us with timidity and inaction, and it is not acceptable to the Father. It will prevent us from being lifted up. We need to remember that for the Christian, God really is at every turn.

Positive Fear

The type of fear, accepted by God and expected by God, is that positive feeling of reverence, respect, and yes, honor, that we offer to the Father. That kind of fear brings about obedience based on a faith that leads to knowledge, wisdom, and innumerable blessings. Righteous living is a product of this type of fear, and the other kind of fear, dread of punishment, recedes as our love for God grows. Perfect love casts out the fear and torment that Satan would have us feel (1 John 4:18).

When I obeyed the gospel as a girl of thirteen, my motivation was a fear of going to hell. As I grew to know God and to seek His favor, that crippling fear was cast out, and the fear which is indicative of acknowledging the awesomeness of our Creator took its place. As my love for the Father grew, so did the right kind of fear.

Yet it was that elementary type of fear that set me on the path to spiritual growth. The prophet Isaiah spoke eloquently about both types of fear. "The Lord of hosts, Him you shall hallow; let Him be your fear, and let Him be your dread" (Isaiah 8:13).

It is truly important to have the appropriate fear for the Lord. When Paul wrote to the church at Ephesus, advising children to obey their parents, he reminded them that the kind of behavior that demonstrates the fear of the Lord would be to their advantage: "That it may be well with you and you may live long on the earth" (Ephesians 6:3). Their days would be prolonged as Solomon had written in those inspired general guidelines for life called Proverbs.

Paul also instructed the church at Corinth that the positive type of fear could complete the process of sanctification. Years ago, one of my public-school students asked me if I had been sanctified. I was taken aback because I had never thought of my Christianity in those terms. Those of us in the Lord's church tend to shy away from that word *sanctification*, yet the apostle Paul wrote in his first letter to the church at Corinth, "But you were washed, but you were sanctified, but you were justified in the name of the Lord Jesus and by the Spirit of our God" (1 Corinthians 6:11). In his second letter to that same congregation, Paul admonished, "Therefore having these promises, beloved, let us cleanse ourselves from all filthiness of the flesh and spirit, perfecting holiness in the fear of God" (2 Corinthians 7:1). When the pursuit of holiness is our goal, God lifts us up. In fact, if we want to see God, we must be holy (Hebrews 12:14).

> We focus on being happy rather than holy.

Choose to Fear God: Be Holy and Be Happy

Sometimes I think that we have, all too often, abandoned the concept of holiness, and we have also forgotten that God has called us unto holiness (1 Thessalonians 4:7). We are more focused on being happy rather than holy, not realizing that it is possible to be both.

The first-century church comprehended the true meaning of the fear of God.

> Then the churches throughout all Judaea and Galilee and Samaria had peace and were edified. And walking in the fear of the Lord and in the comfort of the Holy Spirit, they were multiplied (Acts 9:31).

Solomon wrote that we are refusing wisdom when we do not have the fear of God, and how can God lift us up if we do not fear Him? Wisdom was personified as she spoke the words,

> Then they will call on me, but I will not answer; they will seek me diligently, but they will not find me. Because they hated knowledge and did not choose the fear of the Lord (Proverbs 1:28–29).

King Solomon, in his proverbs, expressed the same idea over and over. The fear of the Lord is a prerequisite for spiritual, emotional, and even physical survival. "In the fear of the Lord there is strong confidence, and His children will have a place of refuge" (Proverbs 14:26). When we fear God, we have access to life everlasting. "The fear of the Lord is a fountain of life, to turn one away from the snares of death" (Proverbs 14:27).

A Sense of Awe, Not Panic

The fear of the Lord is for our own good and well-being. God said so. By inspiration Jeremiah wrote,

> They shall be my people, and I will be their God; then I will give them one heart and one way, that they may fear Me forever, for the good of them and their children after them. And I will make an everlasting covenant with them, that I will not turn away from doing them good; but I will put My fear in their hearts that they will not depart from Me (Jeremiah 32:38–40).

Once again, the fear that is spoken of here is the reverence that we feel for God because of all He has done for us and because of the great love that He has shown to us through the gift of His only begotten Son. This fear is a sense of awe that is based on His magnificence and what we owe Him, not panic which has its origin in what punishment God might dispense. This fear or awe is the feeling of respect and adoration which keeps us in an attitude of obedient homage and praise.

You are not alone, God is within.

—Epictetus

Frequently, even in our assemblies, there is no hush, no sense of God's nearness. No, the church buildings are not holy; the meeting sites have not been sanctified in the same sense as was the tabernacle or the temple of old, but I'm concerned that many of us approach worship in the wrong frame of mind. A large number of us have become gum-chewing, loud-talking, technologically distracted by electronic devices, and unfocused individuals as we take to our pews on the first day of the week. We must reclaim the appropriate type of fear, this awe as we come into the Father's presence.

Awe is not the fear that makes us behave simply because we think someone is looking. Isaiah wrote about that wrong kind of fear.

> Therefore the Lord said: "Inasmuch as these people draw near with their mouths and honor Me with their lips, but have removed their hearts far from Me, and their fear toward Me is taught by the commandment of men" (Isaiah 29:13).

You, Me, and God

We need to fear God always because even when we think that we are totally alone, we should remember that we are not. Of course, we sometimes do tend to forget that God, in His omniscience, always has us under observation. One night, many years ago, all my family had places to be and things to do except for me and my daughter Casey who was four years old. She saw the world from a different viewpoint than that of adults. Casey's perspective was simple and to the point. Rather than saying that we were home by ourselves, she said, "Mama, there is no one here except you, me, and God."

Not many years after the birth of Christ, Epictetus expressed the same idea:

> When you close your doors, and make darkness within, remember never to say that you are alone, for you are not alone, God is within, and your genius is within. And what need have they of light to see what you are doing?

Too often we forget that we are never truly by ourselves, or at least, we don't have to be. We turn our backs on God rather than the reverse. It is we who abandon Him. When we refuse to acknowledge God's presence as a constant in our lives, we lose that fear, the awe, and the respect that "prolongs days."

Honor Him All the Time

All too often we do not even look for God until trouble comes, and then we expect Him to bail us out. The Father is not simply a God of emergency rooms. We should not say God is good only when life is going well for us. God is good all the time, whatever our external circumstances. To blame God for the hardships in life is not only illogical, but it is also an attitude that is probably offensive to the Father.

Good times are enriched whenever we can feel that God is with us and is pleased. True happiness includes God. We should look to God when we are happy, as well as when we are sad or dealing with difficult situations. External conditions should not control our state of mind because, in the end, our relationship with God is all that matters. Our lives should honor God whatever the state of our affairs.

God, Our Rock

The fear that "prolongs days" reminds us that we are not dealing with just anyone. Our God exercises "lovingkindness, judgment, and righteousness in the earth" (Jeremiah 9:24).

Our God is more powerful than tongue can tell.

For behold, He who forms mountains, and creates the wind, who declares to man what his thought is, and makes the morning darkness, who treads the high places of the earth— the Lord God of hosts is His name (Amos 4:13).

Our God is "merciful and gracious, longsuffering, and abounding in goodness and truth, keeping mercy for thousands, forgiving iniquity and transgression and sin" (Exodus 34:6–7).

When we have the right kind of fear toward God, we have in our possession great confidence in Him. Isaiah instructed, "You will keep him in perfect peace, whose mind is stayed on You, because he trusts in You. Trust in the Lord forever, for in Yah, the Lord is everlasting strength" (Isaiah 26:3–4). In the Hebrew language, the words "everlasting strength" actually are indicative of the phrase, "the rock of ages."

> The Father is not simply a God of emergency rooms.

David, the shepherd boy and king, knew that our Father is a Rock upon which we can stand and be lifted up if we have the fear of the Lord God. "And he said, 'The Lord is my rock and my fortress and my deliverer; the God of my strength, in whom will I trust; my stronghold and my refuge'" (2 Samuel 22:2–3).

Moses, the man of God, also understood that our God is a high place in time of trouble. Didn't he discover that fact time and time again in his own life? "For I proclaim the name of the Lord: ascribe greatness to our God. He is the Rock, His work is perfect; for all His ways are justice, a God of truth and without injustice, righteous and upright is He" (Deuteronomy 32:3–4).

When we truly have the right kind of fear toward God, we strive to be obedient to Him. We are not full of our own importance or our own wisdom, but we look to Him for guidance, remembering that just as the fear of the Lord adds days, "the years of the wicked will be shortened" (Proverbs 10:27).

Solomon said that there are exceptions to this standard—to this principle. He acknowledged,

> I have seen everything in my days of vanity: there is a just man who perishes in his righteousness, and there is a wicked man who prolongs his life in his wickedness. Do not be overly righteous, nor be overly wise: why should you destroy yourself? Do not be overly wicked, nor be foolish: why should you die before your time? (Ecclesiastes 7:15–17).

Another favorite scripture of mine is Isaiah 33:6: "Wisdom and knowledge will be the stability of your times, and the strength of salvation; the fear of the Lord is His treasure." God is pleased when we fear Him, when we honor Him with respect and awe and love. Our Father treasures that gift to Him from His children. He said so.

The bottom line is that the fear of the Lord increases our prospects for a happier, longer, more productive life in this world, and it certainly ensures it in the next. When we love and fear God, the stress with which all of us deal daily is lessened. We can proclaim as the psalmist did, "In the multitude of my anxieties within me, Your comforts delight my soul" (Psalm 94:19). We will be lifted up if we fear the Lord.

✤Questions✤

1. Why is having the fear of the Lord an advantage for us?

2. Exactly what is this "fear of the Lord"?

3. Explain 2 Corinthians 7:1.

4. What do we lose if we do not choose the fear of the Lord? (Read Proverbs 14:26–27.)

5. What did Isaiah say was the wrong kind of fear? (Read Isaiah 29:13.)

6. How is God described in Jeremiah 9:24?

7. What does Amos say about God's power? (Read Amos 4:13.)

8. What does Moses say about God in Exodus 34:6–7?

9. Explain why God is "the rock of ages."

10. Discuss the life of Moses and his realization that God is a high place in time of trouble.

✤My Progress✤

What have you learned about the fear of the Lord?

5

Be One Who Wins Souls

"The fruit of the righteous is a tree of life, and he who wins souls is wise." Proverbs 11:30

We need each other. We can accomplish together what we would fail at alone. Solomon knew this. He wrote,

Two are better than one, because they have a good reward for their labor. For if they fall, one will lift up his companion. But woe to him who is alone when he falls, for he has no one to help him up. Again, if two lie down together, then they will keep warm; but how can one be warm alone? Though one may be overpowered by another, two shall withstand him. And a threefold cord is not quickly broken (Ecclesiastes 4:9–12).

Because we do need each other, we should love and care for one another. We should be concerned enough that we want every soul to be won for the Lord Jesus Christ. I have a horror of appearing at judgment and hearing some lost soul say to me the words of James Rowe's thought-provoking hymn, "You

LIFT ME UP

Never Mentioned Him to Me." That will be a serious charge indeed. That beautiful song proclaims a somber indictment:

> You never mentioned Him to me;
> You helped me not the Light to see.
> You met me day by day and knew I was astray;
> Yet you never mentioned Him to me.

Please, dear God, help me to mention Jesus to others. Help me not to fail You.

Am I Kin to God?

When I stand at the judgment seat of Christ (2 Corinthians 5:10), I am going to be much more anxious about the things I neglected to do rather than being overly concerned about a list of wrongdoings on my part. When Jesus described the final judgment in Matthew 25, He spoke of things individuals did not do, such as providing food and drink and hospitality, clothing the needy, and visiting the sick, as well as tending to those in prison. He did not present a tally of overt sins. Will I be able to tell the Lord that my religion was pure and undefiled, that as well as keeping myself unspotted from the world, I cared for orphans and widows (James 1:27)?

Does my life demonstrate that I actually love others? Have I truly been created in Christ Jesus for good works (Ephesians 2:10)?

Jesus continues to think that it is important for us to treat each other well. Yes, our Savior commanded that we love one another (John 15:17), and that love is made manifest when we

58

serve each other, supplying whatever need is present, whether that necessity is spiritual, physical, or emotional.

We can mention Jesus to others each day, not only with our voices, but also with the kind of lives we lead. We mention Him when we help another person. When we smile or lighten someone else's load, we mention Him. We mention Him when we imitate His behavior in our lives. Our kinship to Christ should be evident in every behavior that we exhibit. Can people tell that you are "kin to God"?

> Sometimes I practice avoidance.

Does the good news of Christ consume our hearts the way God's message burned in Jeremiah's heart six hundred years before we were given the gospel? Do we speak as Jeremiah did when he asserted, "But His word was in my heart like a burning fire shut up in my bones; I was weary of holding it back, and I could not" (Jeremiah 20:9)? The prophet had been struck and placed in stocks (Jeremiah 20:2) shortly before he uttered those words. We who are free to speak openly and to live without chains should feel God's Word burning in our hearts and bones, and we should speak out for Jesus.

The word that Jeremiah proclaimed for the Lord was not nearly as glorious as the beautiful message we have been given. Yet Jeremiah said, "Your word was to me the joy and rejoicing of my heart; for I am called by Your name, O Lord God of hosts" (Jeremiah 15:16). Those of us who bear the name of Christ should feel that the gospel is the "joy and rejoicing" of our hearts and minds, and we should share it with others in order to win souls for Him. When we do so, God will lift us up.

Teach Them Diligently

Sharing the gospel may not be politically correct in our day, but we must share anyway. Are you as I am? Sometimes I practice avoidance. I don't want to get into an extended discussion. Or perhaps I'm tired or simply apathetic. I must overcome those obstacles. I must strive to speak a good word for Jesus at every opportunity. Not only that, I must look for opportunities, and I must recognize them when they present themselves.

I am lifted up when I think of Susie, my sweet sister in Christ. I am also embarrassed by my own inaction as a mature Christian when I think of her. Susie, a new citizen of the kingdom, taught Dana, a neighbor in her apartment complex, the good news of Jesus. Dana died only a few months afterward, but Dana went home a child of God because Susie loved her enough to become involved and to teach her the truth.

Sometimes I wonder if we even mention Him to our family members, and if so, how often. Could that be one of the reasons that so many of our young people are leaving the church? Moses directed the people of his day very carefully in this matter.

> And these words which I command you today, shall be in your heart. You shall teach them diligently to your children, and shall talk of them when you sit in your house, when you walk by the way, when you lie down, and when you rise up (Deuteronomy 6:6–7).

Those instructions are very clear; aren't they? We now have the New Testament as well as the Old, and God's plan for us has changed since Moses spoke those words over three thousand years ago, but the principle behind those directions has not changed. If you want someone to learn something, you teach him. You show him. You tell him. You practice the behavior before him, and you do not do it once or twice but day in and day out, regardless of the other activities in which you might be engaged. We are obligated to bring our children up "in the training and admonition of the Lord" (Ephesians 6:4).

❧ Daily Show and Tell

During the summer months, I often provided daycare for two of my grandchildren as they were growing up. It finally occurred to me that I was neglecting a great opportunity to reinforce what they were learning at home and church. Oakley, Gracie, and I began having daily devotionals, and I was amazed at the enjoyment that time together in God's Word provided us. It is to my shame that we did not begin that activity sooner. How can I expect God to lift up my children and grandchildren if I do not attempt to instruct them in His Word?

Since they were babies, Oakley and Gracie have watched me engage in Bible study every morning, but I need to be certain that I am continually speaking of God's love for us as well as showing them the need for studying Scripture.

As a public schoolteacher, I was astounded by the number of children who knew next to nothing about the Bible. Sometimes in literature class we would encounter an allusion to Moses or Noah, and many students did not know who those men were. I had one student who had never heard of Jesus. That sounds incredible; doesn't it? This was right in the middle of the Bible belt, but sadly enough, it is a true incident.

Who we are and what we believe is basically a result of the way that we are brought up or nurtured. Spirituality, at least to a great degree, is learned. Values, or the lack of them, are passed from one generation to the next. Yes, these spiritual and moral standards have to be taught, either directly or indirectly. One does not contract true religion or develop spirituality the way he catches a childhood disease.

The Importance of Where You Worship

Of the greatest importance ultimately is the transmitted characteristic of religious orientation. At the very least, congregations must retain the children of its members if those congregations are to survive. Various studies show that this should be possible. I once took a graduate course on church growth, and research was mentioned that demonstrated that church attendance, religious beliefs, and other behaviors related to religion have high levels of parent-child similarity. I read one study that indicated there is religious continuity through three generations. One is much more apt to change his political leanings than his religious affiliation.

Since too large a percentage of children of Christians are leaving the church once they graduate from high school or college, the research would not appear to be valid for most congregations. Or is it? Could it be that the parents of those children have never actually "bought into" the system which is, in this case, the church? Or could it be that we are seeing this loss of continuity and correlation because these children are the third generation where deviation so often begins? Is the church losing members because its teachings have been weakened or treated with less importance as one generation gives way to another?

If the research is accurate, and I believe it is, the church should be able to experience growth again if the current generation is truly reached with the gospel, if those souls are sincerely won for Christ—if their Christianity is active rather than passive. It was during the 1940s and 1950s that the church grew phenomenally because of missionary zeal. It follows logically that if we can faithfully and consistently teach the current generation, the church should begin to grow again, at least for a period of thirty to forty years.

> Spirituality is not caught like a childhood disease.

Turn Many to Righteousness

How can we hope to be lifted up if we are not working to win souls? We are instructed to teach others and to give those around us the opportunity to hear the good news. Paul wrote, "And how shall they believe in Him of whom they have not heard?" (Romans 10:14).

Before Jesus ascended into heaven, He stressed the importance of the teaching process, directing His disciples to make other disciples, baptizing them and teaching them to observe all the things which He had commanded (Matthew 28:19–20). The purpose of this commandment is to spur us to make disciples or Christians of all nations because the Lord is "not willing that any should perish but that all should come to repentance" (2 Peter 3:9).

God approves of us when we teach others the truth. In his letter to the Christians that were "scattered abroad," James stated, "Let him know that he who turns a sinner from the error of his way will save a soul from death, and cover a multitude of sins" (James 5:20). Most of us would go out of our way to save someone from physical harm or death, yet we sit back apathetically as individuals all around us are dying spiritually every day.

Share His good news and be lifted up.

The message of Daniel compared those who teach others the way of God to stars shining in the sky: "Those who are wise shall shine like the brightness of the firmament, and those who turn many to righteousness like the stars forever and ever" (Daniel 12:3). The word *wise* there in Hebrew alludes to teachers, and each of us should want to teach others or "turn many to righteousness."

We need to follow the example of Jesus who was the Master Teacher. Even His enemies said of Him, "Teacher, we know that You are true, and teach the way of God in truth" (Matthew 22:16). Jesus has not commanded us to do anything that He didn't do Himself. Jesus has been set on high. In fact, "He was received up into heaven, and sat down at the right hand of God" (Mark 16:19). When we share His good news, we also will be lifted up.

— ❧ Questions ❧ —

1. Why do we need each other? (Read Ecclesiastes 4:9–12.)

2. List some ways we can mention Jesus to others every day?

3. How should we be like Jeremiah? What should be our "joy and our rejoicing"?

4. How are values passed from one generation to the next? How did Moses say to do this?

5. Why do you think the church is losing so many young people?

6. Does your own congregation have a history of losing its youth to the world? If so, what can you do about it?

7. Does God want us to teach others? Identify scriptures that command us to teach.

8. What can hide "a multitude of sins"? Why do you think this is so?

9. Does God want all men to be saved? How do you know?

10. What keeps you from sharing the good news about Jesus?

— ❧ My Progress ❧ —

What have you learned about the importance of winning souls?

6

Speak a Good Word

"Anxiety in the heart of man causes
depression, but a good word
makes it glad." Proverbs 12:25

ave you given anyone a good word today? Have you
made someone's heart lighter? Have you caused a friend
to smile? Have you made anybody glad? If not, why not?

Words are so powerful. They can hurt, and they can heal.
They can destroy, and they can renew. They can bring sadness or
joy. They can offer comfort or pain. Bergen Evans said, "Words
are one of our chief means of adjusting to all the situations of
life. The better control we have over words, the more successful our adjustment is likely to be." I want to control my words,
and I want to use them to make others glad that I have spoken.

Develop the "Good Word" Talent

King Solomon, inspired by the Holy Spirit, stated, "A man has
joy by the answer of his mouth, and a word spoken in due season, how good is it!" (Proverbs 15:23).

The prophet Isaiah wrote, "The Lord God has given Me the
tongue of the learned, that I should know how to speak a word
in season to him who is weary" (Isaiah 50:4). This was part of

a prophetic statement concerning the wonderful personality of Jesus, but we should be seeking to have such a tongue as well. How splendid it would be to have the ability to soothe one who is weary, one who is physically or mentally exhausted. How marvelous it would be to give consolation to one who is grieving. How extraordinary it would be to lessen the anguish of a fellow being. That is what a good word can do. Christians should be filled with good words which they use to lighten the burdens of others.

I will be with your mouth, and teach you what you shall say.

—Exodus 4:12

I once knew a woman who really worked at speaking a pleasant word. She was a woman of God who decided that she wanted to do more for the cause of Christ. I watched her grow spiritually. She became willing to lead prayer in our ladies' class, and she wrote poems and articles for a newsletter. Deciding to do more, she began to send notes of encouragement to fellow members. This ministry of hers came about all because she realized that she, too, could speak a good word.

It is truly a gift to be able to communicate with others in such a way that they are helped. Each of us can develop that talent if we set our minds to do so. Do you remember when God told Moses the great plan that He had for Moses' life? Moses was afraid and answered God, "O my Lord, I am not eloquent, neither before nor since You have spoken to Your servant; but I am slow of speech, and slow of tongue" (Exodus 4:10).

God reassured Moses by telling him, "Now therefore, go, and I will be with your mouth, and teach you what you shall say" (Exodus 4:12).

Moses was still not convinced, and God became angry with him. However, the Lord did agree to give Moses some help. "Is not Aaron the Levite your brother? I know that he can speak well" (Exodus 4:14).

Yet if one will read the books of the Bible that give an account of the life of Moses, it is obvious that Moses learned to speak for himself and to offer guidance to others. It can be seen that Moses did not always depend on Aaron to do the talking. In fact, it was quite the contrary.

Neither do we need to depend on others to speak the good words that should be spoken by us. There may not always be an Aaron around.

Pray Good Words

Children give good words so often. When my son Rob was not quite three years old, he said a prayer that startled me, but it was filled with good words, and it made me glad.

As he usually did, he began, "Thank you for my mama and my daddy, and my sissy." Then Rob said, "And thank you for meself, in Jesus' name. Amen."

I do not know if Rob's prayer made God smile, but it brought joy to me. Yet, I was just about to correct his grammar when it occurred to me what a grand thing he had thanked God for—himself, his own happy life-filled little body. I realized, too, after listening to Rob that perhaps my own prayers had become stale and routine. After all, I had not thanked God for "meself" lately. I had not always offered good words to the Father.

Prayers are our good words to God, and even though He doesn't need them to be made glad, those spiritual sacrifices of praise can make our own hearts happy as we offer them to the Lord for His consideration. The writer of Hebrews advised, "Therefore, by Him let us continually offer the sacrifice of praise to God, that is the fruit of our lips, giving thanks to His name" (Hebrews 13:15).

Choose Words That Soothe

If we cannot offer a good word, we do not need to speak at all. Speaking a word out of turn caused Moses to lose his chance of entering the promised land. "They angered Him also at the waters of strife, so that it went ill with Moses on account of them; because they rebelled against His Spirit, so that he spoke rashly with his lips" (Psalm 106:32–33). How many times have I spoken rashly with my lips? I don't want an uncontrolled tongue to keep me from my own promised land of heaven.

We need to be very careful in our choice of words. Robert Southey, the late eighteenth- and early nineteenth-century English poet, noted, "It is with words as with sunbeams—the more they are condensed, the deeper they burn." Another poet of that same era, Sir Walter Scott, wrote,

> O, many a shaft, at random sent,
> Finds a mark the archer little meant!
> And many a word, at random spoken,
> May soothe or wound a heart that's broken.

We should be certain that the words we employ soothe rather than wound. I don't want my words to be shafts driven into the hearts of others to injure them. May my words be a balm that relieves pain or misery. Let my words bring laughter; let my words lift the load another carries, rather than adding to the burdens by which they are already weighed down.

The first part of Proverbs 12:25, which we used as the springboard for this chapter, serves to remind us that anxiety or heaviness of heart can cause an individual depression or sorrow. An encouraging word can have a powerful impact on someone's state of mind. When individuals face failures or challenges of any kind, just knowing that another human being is rooting for them and wanting them to succeed can make all the difference.

> Be certain that your words soothe, rather than wound.

Words Justify or Condemn

In the gospel of Matthew, Jesus had just been teaching about the heart of man when He went on to remark, "But I say unto you that for every idle word men may speak, they will give account of it in the day of judgment" (Matthew 12:36). Our Savior was even more precise when He added, "For by your words you will be justified, and by your words you shall be condemned" (Matthew 12:37). I don't want my words to condemn me; do you?

This same thought which was eloquently expressed by Jesus had been spoken by Solomon through divine inspiration about one thousand years earlier. "Death and life are in the power of the tongue, and those who love it will eat its fruit" (Proverbs 18:21).

James had much to say about the power of the tongue and our need to allow God to have control over the words we utter (James 3:1–12). It is a paradox that something capable of so much good can do so much harm. "Out of the same mouth proceed blessing and cursing. My brethren, these things ought not to be so" (James 3:10).

Think Before You Speak

Assuredly, we need to weigh our spoken thoughts when we give others advice. We need to be certain that we are offering a good word. After my husband Bob died, I struggled to bring up my children alone. I often felt tremendous responsibility in attempting to use good words as I offered counsel to my children. I was not always successful, but as I have grown older, I have learned to evaluate my thoughts a little more thoroughly before I turn them into spoken words.

More years ago than I care to remember, a few weeks before my son left for college, he needed a good word. Rob said to me, "Mother, as I look around at others, it seems to me that so many people are unhappy with their lives and with what they are doing. I think that I will live at home forever and just go for walks in the woods."

Of course, that game plan would never work, but it was an uncertain time for Rob, and he was fearful of making the wrong decisions as he determined the course that his life would take.

All I could do was tell my son to lean on the Lord, that God loved him, and that he should take each day as it came and think things through before acting. I wanted Rob to realize that God takes care of His own, and that He wants to lift us up and set each of us on high, but we have to be His children, and we have to walk in the light (1 John 1:5–7). Those were the best words I could give Rob.

No Words, Just Action

Sometimes the best word is no word at all. In many situations it is actually better to say nothing. Don't tell a newly bereaved widow that you know how she feels. You don't. Even if you are a widow yourself, you still do not know. Every situation is different. If a parent has lost a child to death, if a friend is experiencing a divorce, ponder your words carefully before you speak. Be sparing with advice even if your opinion is asked. Usually your presence is enough.

About the only good thing Job's friends did for him when they heard of his adversity was to show up and be with him. If they had simply left it at that, the friends would have been less likely to incur God's wrath.

> For they had made an appointment together to come and mourn with him, and to comfort him. . . . So they sat down with him on the ground seven days and seven nights, and no one spoke a word to him for they saw that his grief was very great (Job 2:11, 13).

Job's friends simply sat with him for seven days and nights. What a wonderful gesture! But then they spoiled it by speaking thoughtlessly about matters of which they knew very little.

Solomon wrote, "Do not be rash with your mouth, and let not your heart utter anything hastily before God. For God is in heaven, and you on earth; therefore, let your words be few" (Ecclesiastes 5:2). Silence is definitely called for if a considered response or a good word cannot be spoken.

Rash Promises and Oaths

Be careful in making promises. It is better to remain silent than to make a promise you will not be able to fulfill. How many children have had their hearts broken by parents who did not keep a promise to them? Sometimes spoken vows are promises that cannot or perhaps should not be kept. Herod the tetrarch made an oath to the daughter of Herodias who had pleased him with her dance. He promised to give her whatever she might ask. That rash promise cost John the Baptist his life. The king was sorry that he had made that pledge (Matthew 14:9), but John was beheaded nonetheless.

> *Let your words be few.*
>
> —Ecclesiastes 5:2

There are numerous Old Testament warnings about making oaths. For example, Judges 21 describes two rash vows the nation of Israel made, and those oaths caused problems for God's people as they dealt with the rebellious tribe of Benjamin. Who could possibly forget Jephthah's rash vow in Judges 11? Jephthah's daughter paid the price for her father's injudicious words.

74

Do you remember what Jesus said in His sermon on the mount? "But let your 'Yes' be 'Yes' and your 'No,' 'No.' For whatever is more than these is from the evil one" (Matthew 5:37). An inspired writer echoed that thought when he penned, "But above all, my brethren, do not swear, either by heaven or by earth or with any other oath. But let your 'Yes' be 'Yes' and your 'No' 'No,' lest you fall into judgment" (James 5:12).

Words always mean something, and we should not speak without giving due thought to our words. How often have we wanted a "do over" because the words we spoke brought harm or confusion? As Christians, let's strive to make all our words be good, and God will lift us up.

— ⟫Questions⟪ —

1. What will a good word do? (Read Proverbs 15:23.)

2. Explain the power of words. How can one use that power in a positive way?

3. How can we develop the ability to use good words?

4. Why did Moses think that he needed Aaron to speak for him?

5. How are prayers good words?

6. How can the tongue be both an instrument for good and a weapon for evil? (Read James 3:1–12.)

7. Do children seem to know instinctively how to comfort with good words? Explain your answer.

8. What did Jesus say about our words? (Read Matthew 12:36–37.)

9. Describe some instances when it would be better to say nothing at all.

10. List other scriptures that stress the importance of a good word, for example, Proverbs 25:11 and Proverbs 15:1.

My Progress

What have you learned about the importance of a good word?

Acknowledge The Eyes of the Lord

"The eyes of the Lord are in every
place, keeping watch on the evil
and the good." Proverbs 15:3

Charles Colton, a nineteenth-century English cleric, once wrote, "Men will wrangle for religion; write for it; fight for it; die for it; anything but—live for it." That statement is all too often true. Many people believe in God; but when it comes to letting their lives be an example of obedience to Him, well, that's another story.

Rather than acknowledge the fact that nothing escapes God's attention, many individuals seem to think that He is not aware of their actions. Or even worse, they believe that He does not care. These people believe that God is too exalted or too busy to notice their shortcomings, so as long as they don't stray too far, God will overlook what they consider to be minor misdemeanors.

That line of thinking is flawed; God notices all. "The Lord looks from heaven; He sees all the sons of men. From the place of His dwelling He looks on all the inhabitants of the earth" (Psalm 33:13–14). Jehovah knows all, and no matter is too small for His judgment. Since God is aware of even the number of hairs on our heads (Matthew 10:30), it is certain that our daily activities are under His inspection.

The psalmist wrote concerning that attitude of the wicked, "He has said in his heart, 'God has forgotten; He hides His face; He will never see'" (Psalm 10:11). Yet God does see.

The prophet Jeremiah recorded just how complete and universal God's knowledge of events is.

> "Am I a God near at hand," says the Lord, "And not a God afar off? Can anyone hide himself in secret places, so I shall not see him?" says the Lord; "Do I not fill heaven and earth?" says the Lord (Jeremiah 23:23–24).

The psalmist praised God for His goodness and His constant supervision when he said, "Behold, the eye of the Lord is on those who fear Him, on those who hope in His mercy" (Psalm 33:18). That same thought was expressed again when David, the shepherd boy and king, stated, "The eyes of the Lord are on the righteous, and His ears are open to their cry" (Psalm 34:15).

✦ God sees us when we neglect a chance to do a kindness.

✦ God sees us when we take advantage of another's weakness to better ourselves.

✦ God sees us when we cheat—no matter by how small a margin, no matter what activity is involved.

+ God sees us when we lie—no matter what about, no matter to whom, no matter the reason.

+ God sees us when we are determined to get our way, when we use foul means to accomplish a goal.

+ God sees us when we are vindictive, when we want revenge at any cost.

On the other hand, God also sees us when we are good and when we are kind, generous, loving, and forgiving. God's knowledge encompasses our good deeds as well as our bad. It is comforting to realize that God is certainly cognizant of our behavior when we are doing our best to be like Him.

During the days of the Civil War, someone once said to President Abraham Lincoln, "We trust, Sir, that God is on our side." President Lincoln replied, "It is more important to know that we are on God's side." By our daily behavior, both God and the world can tell whose side we are on.

When Jesus was on the earth, He watched people, and He knew their thoughts (Matthew 9:4). He is still watching today. Jesus looked after the needs of others when He walked among men, and if we will accept and obey Him, He will take care of us today.

Great Things He Has Done

Do you remember the man who was possessed of many devils? That poor soul cried out, "What have I to do with You, Jesus, Son of the Most High God?" Yet Jesus lifted this man up when He healed him. In a very real sense, Jesus set him on high. Luke painted a beautiful word picture. "Then they went out to see what had happened, and came to Jesus, and found the man, from whom the demons had departed, sitting at the feet of Jesus, clothed and in his right mind" (Luke 8:28–35). I love that phrase, "in his right mind." It is only Christians who are in their right minds today. It is only Christians who are truly lifted up.

> The eyes of Jesus are penetrating.

After he was healed, the man "went his way and proclaimed throughout the whole city what great things Jesus had done for him." The man was following the instructions of Christ who had told him, "Return to your own house, and tell what great things God has done for you" (Luke 8:39). Have I told others what great things God has done for me? We should always give God the credit for taking care of us and lifting us up.

God's eyes are on us, and He knows whether or not we have gratitude in our hearts. We should not have the attitude of the nine lepers who refused to acknowledge their debt to Jesus. It was when the Samaritan leper returned to offer thanks that Jesus said, "Were there not ten cleansed? But where are the nine? Were there not any found who returned to give glory to God except this foreigner?" (Luke 17:12–18). We need to make certain that our behavior is different from the nine who pleaded for the mercy of Jesus, yet who were not grateful enough to give thanks for that mercy. Part of my daily prayers is a request I make of God that He help me to be more grateful. It is so easy to become complacent and to take God's goodness to us for granted. I don't want to be one of the nine.

⤳ Jesus Sees Your Giving

The eyes of the Son were watching as a poor widow contributed to the offerings given to God. "Now Jesus sat opposite the treasury and saw how the people put money into the treasury. And many who were rich put in much" (Mark 12:41). Jesus commended the widow's attitude toward wealth to His disciples when He told them, "for they all put in out of their abundance, but she out of her poverty put in all that she had, her whole livelihood" (Mark 12:44). That poor widow knew in her heart that "one's life does not consist in the abundance of the things he possesses" (Luke 12:15). The Lord is still watching us today as we give of our means, and He knows whether or not we are giving of our abundance or our poverty.

We should remember that He is not simply watching our attitudes toward our pocketbooks. He is watching to see if we give of our time, our talents, our love, and our joy. His eyes are on us to witness our sharing or displaying our selfishness. It is our choice as to what He will see.

The eyes of Jesus are penetrating, and He knows our thoughts and desires and prejudices as well. Jesus does not judge according to appearance but according to the state of our souls. The Son of God once advised, "Do not judge according to appearance, but judge with righteous judgment" (John 7:24). In other words, He asked us to imitate Him.

Jesus wants to see good things in us, and He gave the world a wonderful gift—a means to be reconciled to God. On one occasion when Jesus went to the synagogue, He read the prophecy of Isaiah concerning Himself.

The Spirit of the Lord is upon Me, because He has anointed Me to preach the gospel to the poor; He has sent Me to heal the brokenhearted, to proclaim liberty to the captives and recovery of sight to the blind, to set at liberty those who are oppressed; to proclaim the acceptable year of the Lord (Luke 4:17–19).

Jesus told His listeners that the scripture was fulfilled that day. Even now, Jesus will heal our broken hearts and bring us deliverance in order that God might cast His eyes on us and be pleased.

Will He Find Us Watching?

Just as God watches us, we are commanded to look for certain things.

✦ We are told to watch for wisdom. Wisdom personified tells us,

Hear instruction and be wise, and do not disdain it. Blessed is the man who listens to me, watching daily at my gates, waiting at the posts of my doors. For whoever finds me finds life, and obtains favor from the Lord; but he who sins against me wrongs his own soul; all those who hate me love death (Proverbs 8:33–36).

✦ We are told to watch for the return of Jesus.

Watch therefore, for you do know not when the master of the house is coming—in the evening, at midnight, at the crowing of the rooster, or in the morning—lest, coming suddenly, he find you sleeping. And what I say to you I say to all: Watch! (Mark 13:35–37).

We don't want Jesus to return and find us unprepared. He will have been watching whether we have or not.

Calling on God in fervent and sincere petitions concerning our needs and honest expressions of praise and thanksgiving will help us to watch. Peter knew this. "But the end of all things is at hand; therefore be serious and watchful in your prayers" (1 Peter 4:7).

Use God's Strength

Because God is watching and knows our true feelings, we need to train ourselves to live by faith in the Son of God and not by faith in self. We need to remember that we can do nothing by our own strength. This has been a problem for me in times past. I have always tended to think, perhaps almost subconsciously, "Well, God, You know how tough I am. You can help me if You want to, but I can pretty well handle the situation." I often found myself asking God for help but then attempting to tell Him what form that aid should be.

Be serious and watchful in your prayers.

—1 Peter 4:7

It has only been as I have grown older that I have truly learned to lean on God and to realize that it is my God who is strong and not I.

Yes, sometimes I am a slow learner. It took the death of a husband, having to nurture three children as a single parent, and developing chronic health issues to make me realize just how much I need the Father. I came to know that reliance on God is so much superior to relying on self. Depending on

83

the Father makes life much less difficult. Later on, marriage to a new husband, who was also the father of two daughters, would cause me to focus even more on my need for God's direction in my life.

God is watching, and He will lift up those who do good, who obey Him, and who are always striving to understand His will for them. Paul told us that it is possible to understand that will. "Therefore do not be unwise, but understand what the will of the Lord is" (Ephesians 5:17). Let us always work to do His good will while He watches us and longs to lift us up.

— Questions —

1. How do we demonstrate that we truly believe in God? How does obedience demonstrate faith?

2. Is any matter too small for God's judgment? How do you know? (Read Matthew 10:30.)

3. Can anyone hide from God? (Read Psalm 33:18 and Psalm 34:15.)

4. Just how much does God's knowledge encompass? List scriptures that support your answer.

5. Why is it important to have a grateful heart? (Read Luke 17:11–19 for a lesson on gratitude.)

6. What are some things that we should watch for as we live the Christian life?

7. How will prayer and thanksgiving help us to be watchful?

8. Are any of us ever truly self-sufficient? Explain your answer.

9. Can we know God's will? (Read Ephesians 5:17.)

 **My Progress**

What have you learned about the omniscience and omnipresence of God?

Practice Being Merry

"All the days of the afflicted are evil,
but he who is of a merry heart has
a continual feast." Proverbs 15:15

A merry heart is truly a wonderful character trait to develop. Depression has become commonplace, even among members of the Lord's church. This condition may be of physiological origin or a side effect of some problem or tragedy in one's life. However, all too often, depression occurs because we have not cultivated a merry heart, because we have not determined within our souls that we are going to approach every event in our lives with a positive attitude.

A cheerful, optimistic heart is a great treasure indeed. It has become something of a cliché, but Christians actually ought to be able to take lemons and make lemonade. Romans 8:28 was not included in Scripture as an afterthought. All things really can work to our good when we are called according to His purpose. A Christian should experience joy regardless of circumstances. A person whose happiness depends on external factors is an eventual candidate for despair, because sooner or later everyone will experience some of the miseries that come with living in this world. In my own life, I have pledged whatever the years may bring or however my circumstances may change that I will choose joy.

Be Giving, Not Grabbing

When our children were young, there was a window through which sunlight streamed into the kitchen. For a little while each day, a patch of light appeared on the refrigerator door. I can still see our daughter Casey, just a toddler, trying to grab hold of that patch of sunshine. Of course, when she would reach out to touch it, her shadow made the sunlight disappear. Even when Casey would approach it from the side of the appliance, she was still unable to capture the sunbeams. The baby could not figure out the phenomenon. The light was there; she could see it; but it wasn't hers to hold in her chubby little hands.

That is the way happiness is. We can't always grasp it even if we think we see it. We have to work and wait and watch and let it touch us, just as the sunlight touched the refrigerator door. We can't take happiness by force. It comes gently or not at all. Happiness is a condition that is quite elusive to some individuals because they are busy grabbing rather than giving.

Then, too, there are some folks who say, "Well, if I could just have so and so, I'd be happy," or "If I can just do this, I won't ask for anything else." That kind of thinking won't work. A friend of mine put it this way, "That old dog won't hunt." We have to be happy as we are now and not as we wish we could be. I once saw a poster that stated, "Happiness is not a station you arrive at, but a manner of traveling." If, as we live day by day, we are not reasonably content, something is wrong. As was noted in a previous chapter, material things and other people might bring us joy temporarily, but they won't repair a damaged life.

⮞ Happiness Test

Happiness is not something found in worldly possessions, nor is it a quality that someone can bestow. Happiness is a by-product of a meaningful, useful existence. Paradoxically, happiness is often found while we are busy looking for something else.

> Are you busy grabbing, rather than giving?

God cannot lift a person up if she does not have the right attitude toward the things that happen to her. There are several questions you might ask yourself to determine whether you are basically a happy person and whether you have a merry heart and are participating in that continual feast of which Solomon wrote.

1. *Do you smile more often than you frown?* I once read that a child laughs or smiles around four hundred times a day, while an adult laughs or smiles around twenty-five times a day. Perhaps that is another reason Jesus said, "Assuredly, I say to you, unless you are converted and become as little children, you will by no means enter the kingdom of heaven" (Matthew 18:3). I need to learn to be as instinctively joyous as little children are. I need to laugh more often. Recently, I heard a lady speak about a friend of hers. She said, "That man may be happy, but he forgot to let his

face know." Have you forgotten to let your face know? How frequent are your smiles?

2. *Do you like yourself?* That is a crucial question. Are you content with the one you see in the mirror? If you met you, would you like you? Are you pleased with the person you are now? If not, what are you going to do about it?

When my granddaughter Gracie was eleven years old, she gave me a gift that she had purchased with her own funds. The present was a poster which I framed and placed in my sunroom, a place where I spend a great deal of my time. The unsigned words on the poster gave me a new definition of the emotion under discussion. "Happiness is when what you think, what you say, and what you do are in perfect harmony." If what I'm thinking, saying, and do- ing are not in alignment, how can I hope to be happy? I need to strive to emulate the behavior recommended by Gracie's poster.

There are several other queries that you can use to gauge your happiness.

✦ Are you needed by anyone?

✦ Do you look forward to tomorrow, or do you dread each new day?

✦ Are your dreams still alive?

✦ Do you have love in your heart?

✦ Do you feel close to God?

✦ Do you have a personal relationship with His blessed Son?

Because it seems to be a buzz phrase of various religious groups, sometimes we in the church shy away from that thought of a personal relationship with Jesus. But in order to be happy, I need to feel comfortable in His presence. To enjoy true happiness, I need to spend time with Jesus—reading and reading again those blessed Gospels and savoring the words He left behind for us. I need to walk in the Savior's steps.

Life Isn't Fair

Sometimes we have difficulty being happy because of the inequities in this world. Injustice is widespread, yet many of us refuse to accept the fact that life is not fair. God never promised that it would be. Don't buy into a false prosperity gospel or the false notion that the Christian walk is a stroll through a rose garden. The prosperity gospel is a lie Satan promotes. Remember what we read in an earlier chapter. God has promised all we need, not all we want (Philippians 4:19). Even though the Lord truly is our shepherd, we might have to travel rough ground to reach those green pastures.

Although it takes most young children several years to realize that this world is filled with unfairness and favoritism, adults should realize this fact and be able to cope without letting it interfere unduly with their sense of well-being or happiness. To put it in today's vernacular, we should admit to ourselves that "life's not always all that it's cracked up to be." In words of still more modern slang, "Get over it!"

In many ways I led a sheltered life. Until I was about eleven years old, I thought all adults were kind, honest people. I thought that justice always ruled and that everyone would be treated equally. Yes, I was truly innocent about the evils in this quagmire we call the world.

I felt that people were divided into two groups—those who went to church and those who didn't. Really bad people were called crooks, and they murdered or robbed just for the fun of it—not accidentally or because they might be hungry.

"But that's not fair, Mother!"

I believed that people were poor because they didn't have an education and didn't want one. I thought the best way to get rich was to get a college degree. It took me about twenty years to learn the truth about that.

As a child, I believed all people would like me if I liked them first. I eventually discovered that was not true either. Some people seem to be born hating and doing evil, often without understanding why they behave the way they do. David knew this. It was he who wrote, "The wicked are estranged from the womb; they go astray as soon as they are born, speaking lies" (Psalm 58:3).

My own children also had to learn the things that took me so long to realize. It took my quiet, sensitive Chris many years to learn of the deceit and cruelty that all too often are found in our world. Chris, a military wife and mother of two young adults, still manages to smile her way through life, even though her husband has been deployed to the Middle East five times and to Africa once, because she possesses a merry heart.

Realistic matter-of-fact Rob has always accepted any unfair facts of life rather quickly. I remember once when he was just a little boy he asked for an ice cream cone. He wanted one just like those pictured on the box of cones. I explained to him that the cones in the box did not have smiling candy faces like the ones pictured on the outside of the carton.

"Oh," he said as he accepted the ice cream cone that I gave to him. Rob discovered at an early age what the poet Longfellow once wrote: "Things are never what they seem." My son used the word *oh* many times before he became a man. Yet Rob has always had a merry heart, and he has coped with the partiality of this life even during the time he was a trauma nurse and saw much that would make anyone sad.

My youngest child Casey was the one who said most often, "But that's not fair, Mother." Understanding the words of our Lord, "for He makes His sun rise on the evil and on the good, and sends rain on the just and on the unjust" (Matthew 5:45), was difficult for her to accept. It took her longer to learn what her siblings had mastered, but she, too, has learned to partake of a continual feast as she continues to cultivate a merry heart, in spite of what the world throws her way. Casey is also a nurse and uses the gift of a cheerful heart to bring a little sunshine into the lives of others. Due to the death of their father while they were still young, all three of my children have learned that it takes effort to maintain a cheerful heart in adverse circumstances.

We all need balance in our lives. It is difficult to thrive emotionally if we do not have enough positive experiences to outweigh the bad or disillusioning ones that come our way, but it is still possible to flourish if we keep merry hearts. We must choose to grow in spite of the unfairness of this existence.

➤ Don't Give in to Misery

There are many circumstances that could cause us to falter in our quest to have joyous hearts. After a bout of Lyme disease, which went undiagnosed for months, I developed several health issues, and I had trouble maintaining a positive attitude. In fact, I was giving in to misery. The neurological damage that I sustained changed my life forever, making chronic pain and fatigue my constant companions. Although I prayed for better health, I came to realize that my physical problems were permanent.

> Shoes in hand, I was locked inside the closet.

Eventually, I began to take encouragement from the apostle Paul's attitude toward dealing with his thorn in the flesh. By inspiration, Paul wrote, "Therefore I take pleasure in infirmities, in reproaches, in needs, in persecutions, in distresses, for Christ's sake. For when I am weak, then I am strong" (2 Corinthians 12:10). Regardless of his difficulties, Paul had a cheerful heart. Why couldn't I have one too? I needed also to remember the words of our Lord to Paul, "My grace is sufficient for you, for My strength is made perfect in weakness" (2 Corinthians 12:9).

It took me a long time to opt to be happy in spite of my problems, but happiness is a choice, and I have chosen joy and contentment rather than despondency and regret because of the limitations to my daily existence. I tell Ellen, my walking buddy, that we are going to be pounding the pavement for many years to come, even if we have to use walkers with those little cut-in-half tennis balls on the legs.

The Gift of Laughter

Humor adds so much to our lives as we make our way from one day to the next. During our life together, my husband Bob did so much to give me a merry heart. He could always make me laugh even if I was determined to be unhappy over some event. Decades ago, when I was on a rampage over the fact that Bob had left a pair of his shoes in the dining room for the umpteenth time, he was really in good form.

Aggravated over such a minor thing, I picked up his shoes and asked if he would allow me to show him something. Bob walked with me to the end of the hall, and I opened a closed door.

"This is a closet," I told him, "a cubicle and a receptacle for various items of clothing. I would appreciate your using it. Your shoes belong in here."

Almost before I had finished speaking, I found myself, with shoes in hand, locked inside the closet. It was dark in there, and I didn't like it a bit, yet I could not keep from laughing. After Bob released me from my temporary prison, I decided that he could keep his shoes anywhere he wanted to, and I knew that I would end up smiling about it simply by remembering the time that he shut me and his shoes up in the closet. I also reminded myself, "Where no oxen are, the trough is clean" (Proverbs 14:4), and there were many times after Bob died that I would have given a great deal to be able to pick up his shoes.

Since Bob's death, I have recalled many humorous incidents that he engineered, and my heart has been made merry again. Once during his final stay at Vanderbilt, he donned a pair of Groucho Marx glasses, mustache and all, and hid under the sheets. I sat quietly in a corner of the hospital room, and as Dr. Wolfe and his residents made their rounds that morning, they had quite a surprise when they pulled back the bed linens. The medical professionals left the room chuckling, and I'm certain they smiled more than once before the day was over. When Bob died, that wonderful man left such a marvelous gift of laughter behind. Each of us should be laughing, happy individuals who help others to have a merry heart.

Reasons for a Happy Heart

We should possess merry hearts because we, as Christians, are without blame.

> Blessed be the God and Father of our Lord Jesus Christ, who has blessed us with every spiritual blessing in the heavenly places in Christ, just as He chose us in Him before the foundation of the world, that we should be holy and without blame before Him in love (Ephesians 1:3–4).

Because I belong to Jesus, I am without blame. That should make me very happy indeed.

Yes, we should have merry hearts because righteousness reigns in our lives. "For if by one man's offense death reigned through the one, much more those who receive abundance of grace and of the gift of righteousness will reign in life through the One, Jesus Christ" (Romans 5:17). Even though I am not righteous through my own merit, because of the blood of my Savior and my acceptance of His wonderful gift of grace and salvation, I am counted as righteous. That fact alone should certainly make me very happy.

We should be happy because we have redemption and forgiveness of sins. "In Him we have redemption through His blood, the forgiveness of sins, according to the riches of His grace" (Ephesians 1:7).

We should have merry hearts because God is always going to be with us unless we push Him away and cease to walk in the light (1 John 1:7). We should be happy because we don't have to doubt God or wonder whether or not He loves us. He has already proved that He does (John 3:16).

> We cannot be happy unless we are creating happiness for others.

We should especially be of a glad heart because we have chosen to allow Christ to live in us. God gives us freedom of choice, but when we obeyed the gospel, Christ became a part of us. There is the idea of that personal relationship again. "I have been crucified with Christ; it is no longer I who live, but Christ lives in me; and the life which I now live in the flesh I live by faith in the Son of God, who loved me, and gave Himself for me" (Galatians 2:20).

George Bernard Shaw once wrote, "We have no more right to consume happiness without producing it than to consume wealth without producing it." I think he made a valid point. In reality, we cannot truly be happy unless we are creating happiness for others also. God lifts those up who have a happy, merry heart.

— ❧ Questions ❧ —

1. Does happiness just happen? If not, how can we find it?

2. Are material possessions necessary for happiness? Prove your answer.

3. Can financial prosperity sometimes be an obstacle to happiness? Is this also true of poverty? Cite scriptures to support your ideas.

4. Why isn't life fair? (Read Matthew 5:45.)

5. Why should we have merry hearts?

6. Who is without blame? (Read Ephesians 1:4.)

7. How can we have the gift of righteousness? (Read Romans 5:17.)

8. How do we have redemption and forgiveness of sins? (Read Ephesians 1:7.)

9. What are other reasons that we should be of a glad heart?

10. What are some things that you can do in your own life to ensure that you have a merry heart?

— ❧ My Progress ❧ —

What have you learned about the importance of cultivating a merry heart?

9

Pray the Prayer Of the Upright

"The sacrifice of the wicked is an abomination to the Lord, but the prayer of the upright is His delight." Proverbs 15:8

Solomon expressed this thought in another way as he spoke of a larger group of individuals. "Righteousness exalts a nation, but sin is a reproach to any people" (Proverbs 14:34). During my lifetime, I have seen drastic changes in what is acceptable and approved in our culture. Our modern civilization has lost its sense of shame. I doubt that Sodom and Gomorrah could have been any worse than our own nation as far as the moral behavior of most of its citizens is concerned.

Pray for Our Country

The media and Hollywood actually celebrate and promote that which God finds abominable. In the area encompassing the cities of Sodom and Gomorrah, only one godly family was located. Sadly, the Lord's church in the United States is not experiencing the growth that it once did. Could it be that there are fewer and fewer godly families in America today? Too many have bought into Satan's lie of political correctness and the belief that it is better for one to act on emotions, illicit desire, or whatever feels good at the moment, rather than striving to live spiritual, moral lives or making any effort to please God. Far too many people live as though God does not actually exist. Christians are often the subject of ridicule or disdain by the mainstream media.

Christians, those who are "upright," as the writer of Proverbs put it, may be in the world, but they should not be of it. We should keep ourselves apart from the evil around us. At the same time, we should pray both privately and publicly for ourselves and for others. Paul wrote Timothy concerning this theme.

> Therefore I exhort first of all that supplications, prayers, intercessions, and giving of thanks be made for all men, for kings and all who are in authority, that we may lead a quiet and peaceable life in all godliness and reverence. For this is good and acceptable in the sight of God our Savior, who desires all men to be saved and to come to the knowledge of the truth (1 Timothy 2:1–4).

A Tale of Two Plagues

Many years ago when I was a columnist for a local paper, I wrote a brief essay about the downward spiral America is taking, and my little parable seems even more relevant now than it did then.

Once upon a time there was a country—a very rich, beautiful country. The land was unusually fertile. There were great farms, luxurious forests, imposing mountains, and many clean, pure streams and rivers. The country was truly blessed with an abundance of resources, including a productive, hard-working population.

In that country (once upon a time), men helped one another. Each was more or less his brother's keeper. No one would knowingly allow a fellow being to suffer from hunger or cold or even a lack of friendship. Honesty was a virtue of a majority of the people. Recreation and entertainment, for the most part, were of an innocent nature. The human body was an object of care and respect rather than one for display or exploitation. The family unit was of great importance. Education was held in high esteem. All this was once upon a time, of course.

And it seemed that the "Great All Father" watched over that country and its people. There was great prosperity, and the potential for growth seemed limitless (once upon a time).

But something happened. In some history books it is said that two plagues struck. One of the diseases was called "Apathy," and the other was labeled "Excessive Self-Interest." I myself believe that it was really a third condition called "Turning from God." Both the country and the people changed, and not for the better.

A lack of concern for others soon became a common symptom of practically everyone. The majority became interested only in themselves—in their own needs, in their own problems. Waste and misuse of resources by the people of that country began the process of destroying the natural environment and using up the land.

The citizens of that country stopped speaking up for what they thought was right. It seemed easier and safer to remain silent. The crime rate rose. Interpretation and enforcement of the laws of the land became less strict. The institutions of marriage and the home began to deteriorate. Children were given freedom to behave as they pleased. People turned to drugs and pornography. They forgot God.

I tried to remember the name of that country, which, as in the case with other civilizations, was created and mightily developed before going into gradual decline and dying. It may have been ancient Egypt. It could have been Greece or Rome. Perhaps it was Israel. Or it just might have been the United States of America. Once upon a time there was a country . . .

Pray Specifically

Of course, many times we as Christians can do nothing but helplessly watch and pray as our country becomes more and more ungodly. Let's pray specifically for our country's morality.

Satan has undoubtedly cheered at the ruling of the Supreme Court concerning several moral issues.

1. The government continues to allow the killing of unborn babies at the rate of about four thousand a day, and hardened criminals are often better protected by the law than their victims. Even certain species of animals are offered greater protection under the law than unborn babies. My husband Mark owns a wildlife control business. Because of laws that shield them, he is not allowed to euthanize snakes or bats, but the same civil authority that shelters wildlife allows unborn infants to be murdered routinely. A law passed in January 2019 in New York makes it legal to abort full-term children or to deny those babies aid if born alive. Third trimester abortion is legal in Oregon, and Vermont is considering such legislation. God cannot be pleased. How long will He allow this to continue?

2. The institution of marriage has been made into a travesty by those who dishonor the plan devised by God. It is both sad and difficult to believe that we live in a country whose government sanctions and promotes same-sex unions.

3. A 2018 Gallup Poll estimates that 4.5 percent of American adults identify as lesbian, gay, bisexual, or transgender. That works out to more than 11 million of America's 325.7 million population (NBC News.com). Yet this small percentage has so influenced our society with their lobbyists and supporters that God's ordained plan for marriage has been made a mockery. God cannot be pleased with us as a nation.

Yet we, as Christians, constantly need to endeavor to be acceptable to God. We must strive toward righteousness. If Lot and his family were living among us, we would not want his family to be the only one approved of God.

Purge Iniquity from Your Heart

We desire God to hear our prayers so that it will continue to be well with us in order that ultimately we will be lifted up. I love the words of the unnamed psalmist,

> Come and hear, all you who fear God, and I will declare what He has done for my soul. I cried to Him with my mouth, and He was extolled with my tongue. If I regard iniquity in my heart, the Lord will not hear. But certainly God has heard me; He has attended to the voice of my prayer. Blessed be God, who has not turned away my prayer, nor His mercy from me! (Psalm 66:16–20).

We need to be certain that, like the psalmist, we are striving to purge iniquity from our hearts. It is then that God will hear us and lift us up. We need to be upright in spirit if we want Him to listen to us. Solomon knew "the Lord is far from the wicked, but He hears the prayer of the righteous" (Proverbs 15:29).

On many occasions, David longed for God's help in order that he should know the way to go. David truly wanted to be lifted up even though he, as the rest of us sometimes do, allowed the desires of the flesh to get in his way. David requested of God, "Cause me to hear Your lovingkindness in the morning, for in You do I trust; cause me to know the way in which I should walk, for I lift up my soul to You" (Psalm 143:8).

Psalm 143:10 is also a good prayer for those who are attempting to live in a manner pleasing to God. David requested, "Teach me to do Your will, for You are my God; Your Spirit is good. Lead me in the land of uprightness."

Pray and Don't Lose Heart

Jesus said that men ought always to pray and not lose heart (Luke 18:1). I don't want to lose heart or lack faith in what God is willing to do for me. I want to always be constant in prayer (1 Thessalonians 5:17). The apostle Paul reminded the church in Rome of the importance of steadfast prayer (Romans 12:12). However, it is the prayer of the righteous in heart that God heeds. "The effective, fervent prayer of a righteous man avails much" (James 5:16). We can't live selfishly for ourselves and then expect God to listen to us.

All things—not some things—work together for good for those who are Christians, for those who are of an upright heart. "And we know that all things work together for good to those who love God,

> If I regard iniquity in my heart, the Lord will not hear.
>
> —Psalm 66:18

to those who are the called according to His purpose" (Romans 8:28). That concept is hard to grasp sometimes, but God said it and it has to be true. My young husband's death, my own chronic illness—all things can work for my good if I continue to allow God to lift me up. God is good all the time, not just those times when life seems to be without problems. His goodness should guide our lives regardless of our circumstances or the problems we may encounter. A quote often attributed to C. S. Lewis says, "Life with God is not immunity from difficulties, but peace in difficulties."

When we are righteous in heart, we are obedient in spirit as well. As a result of our obedience to the gospel, we who once had no hope and were without God are made close to God. Scripture says so, and I believe it.

> At that time you were without Christ, being aliens from the commonwealth of Israel and strangers from the covenants of promise, having no hope, and without God in the world. But now in Christ Jesus you who once were far off have been brought near by the blood of Christ (Ephesians 2:12–13).

Don't those two verses contain some of the most beautiful thoughts in the Bible?

Yes, God will lift each of us up and draw us close to Him if we approach Him with an upright, cleansed heart made possible through the blood of His blessed Son. Our prayer can then be His delight.

Questions

1. Whose prayers are a delight to God?

2. What does righteousness do for a nation? What will sin cause?

3. For whom should we pray? (Read 1 Timothy 2:1–4.)

4. What causes a nation to have serious problems?

5. How can we as a nation or as individuals be acceptable to God? Support your response with scriptural references.

6. According to Proverbs 15:29, whose prayers will God hear?

7. How is it possible that all things work together for good for the Christian? Explain your answer.

8. How do we gain hope and draw nigh to God? (Read Ephesians 2:12–13.)

My Progress

What have you learned about the prayers of the righteous?

10

Accept That Safety Is of the Lord

"The horse is prepared for the day of battle,
but deliverance is of the Lord." Proverbs 21:31

To whom are we looking for our deliverance and safety? How many of us depend on ourselves and on the physical preparation we make for dealing with this life, rather than looking to God for survival and protection? *Safety,* or as the Hebrew word really means, *victory,* is of the Lord.

The sweet psalmist David wrote, "The Lord is my light and my salvation; whom shall I fear? The Lord is the strength of my life; of whom shall I be afraid?" (Psalm 27:1). The Lord can be the strength of our lives also.

In 1834, in a sermon titled "Wisdom and Innocence," John Henry Newman stated,

> May He support us all the day long till the shades lengthen, and the evening comes, and the busy world is hushed, and the fever of life is over, and our work is done. Then in His mercy, may He give us a safe lodging and a holy rest, and peace at the last (NewmanReader.org).

Even though I cannot agree with or accept many of New-man's denominational teachings, I love his imagery in this instance. The Lord will support us until night, or as is really meant, death comes and "the fever of life is over." God will give us a "safe lodging," "a holy rest," and "peace at the last" if we will only look to Him in obedience and allow Him to lift us up.

Paul observed that it is obedience that makes us just or holy before God. "Do you not know that to whom you present yourselves slaves to obey, you are that one's slaves whom you obey, whether of sin leading to death, or of obedience leading to righteousness?" (Romans 6:16).

How many of us have felt as David did when troubles come into our lives as they did into his? David cried from the very core of his being, "Attend to my cry, for I am brought very low" (Psalm 142:6). Undoubtedly, this statement was made during the time that David was on the run from the wrath of Saul. Yet David placed his trust in God, and he was lifted up.

On the Run, Yet Set on High

Sometimes we are on the run, not from an angry king as David was, but from pain, from sorrow, and from the emptiness that may fill our lives. It is then, as always, that we need to place our trust in God as David did.

Our friends may offer security or safety for a while. Friend-ship is truly a wonderful thing. Still, friends sometimes fail us but God never will. Companions may even tire of us, especially if our problems prove to be a drain on the relationship. Solomon wrote, "Seldom set foot in your neighbor's house, lest he become weary of you and hate you" (Proverbs 25:17).

As was mentioned in an earlier chapter, my biggest problem has always been that I attempt to handle everything myself. When troubles come, I seem predisposed to plow through them on my own, when I should be asking the Lord to make a way for me. I tend to forget that it has always been God who has given me strength to deal with pain, with poverty, with sickness, with death, with every difficulty. Are you sometimes like that?

> Friends sometime fail us, but God never will.

David wrote, "O God, You are more awesome than Your holy places. The God of Israel is He who gives strength and power to His people. Blessed be God!" (Psalm 68:35). It is God who gives us strength, who makes victory or safety possible. David knew the sense of security and well-being that comes from trusting in God. "I will both lie down in peace, and sleep; for You alone, O Lord, make me dwell in safety" (Psalm 4:8).

Strength through Persecution: Avoid the Middle of the Road

Even though safety is of the Lord, this world is not always a secure place for the Christian. John A. Shedd once wrote, "A ship in harbor is safe, but that is not what ships are built for." A person who follows Christ cannot constantly reside in the church building or her home. She has to get out among others to do the Lord's work. Danger exists out there. Remember, Paul wrote, "Yes, and all who desire to live godly in Christ Jesus will suffer persecution" (2 Timothy 3:12). That verse always grabs my attention and makes me ponder about persecution, or the lack of it, in my life. The thought sometimes occurs to me that if I am not suffering persecution in some form or fashion, then perhaps my life is not as godly as it should be.

There will be periods of uncertainty or discomfort, either physical or mental or both, if we are striving for heaven and trying to take others with us. Anytime one takes a stand, difficulties arise, but the Christian will also have problems if she doesn't commit herself wholeheartedly to the cause of Christ—if she doesn't have the strength to stand up for what she believes. Sitting on the fence is fine for birds but not for Christians. Robert Frost, a renowned poet, commented, "The middle of the road is where the white line is—and that's the worst place to drive." If we are not soldiers for Christ on a daily basis, how can we possibly believe that we are actually in His army? Too many of us take unauthorized furloughs, and we leave behind those weapons listed in Ephesians 6.

Grow in Leaps of Faith

The medical profession warns us often of behaviors that will threaten our health or physical well-being, but I submit to you that living in general is hazardous to one's health. Yet we should not choose safety at the expense of the adventure of living or the joy life can hold. If we take no risks, it is probable that very little will be gained. George E. Woodberry said, "The willingness to take risks is our grasp of faith." It just might be possible to avoid danger by hiding from life, but what would we have accomplished? Just think what we would miss as far as the wonder of life is concerned.

In my own case, I think how much I would have missed if I had not entered into a second marriage. It took a great leap of faith to remarry after my husband Bob's death, but my second husband Mark is also a Christian, and God has blessed our union more than I could imagine.

One of my favorite hobbies is reading British murder mysteries of the "Golden Age" which were written between World War I and World War II, and I'm constantly on the lookout for those old books, most of which are out of print. On occasion some of the better authors have their characters make remarkable statements. In one of Michael Innes' novels, a detective tells another character, "For it is a denial of life to decline the richness of experience just because in the end, there may be a bill to pay" (Innes 20). Those are wise words for a Christian who is walking in the light. If we aren't willing to take well-considered risks or to make difficult decisions that are in accordance with God's Word, we will be unable to grow in all the ways that matter.

Don't Worry; Be Happy

We don't need to be unmindful of the consequences of our deeds, yet it is all right to love, to laugh, to enjoy life without fear of what may be down the road, because ultimately, if we are God's children, the Lord will lift us up. In the meantime, He will be with us if we are living in accordance with His will. The bill that is due has already been paid by our blessed Savior.

I think that must be what Jesus was telling us when He said, "Therefore do not worry about tomorrow, for tomorrow will worry about its own things. Sufficient for the day is its own trouble" (Matthew 6:34).

I also like the way Henry David Thoreau expressed the idea of dismissing anxiety about dangers and risks which are a part of life that we cannot avoid. Thoreau wrote,

> I saw a delicate flower had grown up two feet high between the horses' path and the wheel track. . . . An inch more to the right or left had sealed its fate, or an inch higher. And yet it lived and flourished . . . and never knew the danger it incurred. It did not borrow trouble nor invite an evil fate by apprehending it (Thoreau 66).

Safe and Sound—or Not?

Some of the most comforting adjectives in the Bible are spoken by Jesus in the parable of the prodigal son. One of the servants told the elder son, "Your brother has come, and because he has received him safe and sound, your father has killed the fatted calf" (Luke 15:27). What beautiful words those are—safe and sound. Oh, that all men and women could be safe and sound on judgment day! Only God the Father through our obedient belief in His blessed Son, the Lord Jesus Christ, can provide that ultimate safety, that final victory, and sadly, countless individuals still reject that security. They are repudiating the status of being safe and sound.

It is especially sad when those we love are not safe in this life, but it is horrible indeed to realize that they are not safe in the world to come. Some of the saddest words penned in the

Old Testament are those of the prophet Jeremiah: "The harvest is past, the summer is ended, and we are not saved!" (Jeremiah 8:20). Several years ago, I spoke of the good news of Jesus to a friend who knew what he should do but simply refused to obey. I sent him a card, and I quoted those poignant words of Jeremiah. At that time, the verse did not persuade my friend, but I learned later that he told his wife, "At least she cares; she hasn't given up on me." Eventually, my friend did obey the gospel.

"Is the young man Absalom safe?"

Do you remember the account of Absalom's rebellion against his father David? Near the end of that sad tale of a son's disobedience and disrespect for his father who was also his king, David asked two different servants. "Is the young man Absalom safe?" (2 Samuel 18:29, 32). David would have been better occupied worrying about Absalom's spiritual safety rather than his physical well-being.

The same is true of us as parents today. Some unknown wise person once said, "Going to church doesn't make you a Christian any more than going into a garage makes you a car." Our children must see that we trust God enough to do what He says, and they must realize that we love Jesus to such an extent that we allow Him to live in us.

We go to extremes to provide security of a physical nature, but too often we neglect spiritual safety. I desperately want God to lift me up, but I want my children and grandchildren, my friends, and all those I love to be lifted up with me also.

More than anything, I want them to know God and His plan for their lives. I want them to know, too, that safety is of the Lord.

— ❧Questions❧ —

1. To whom should we look for safety? Why?

2. Is obedience necessary for safety? Does obedience make us righteous?

3. In what manner are we sometimes on the run as David was?

4. Can our friends offer us security? Why or why not?

5. Can we attain safety by ourselves? Why or why not? (Read Psalm 4:8.)

6. Why is the world not always a safe place for Christians?

7. Have you ever suffered persecution? If so, in what way? (Read 2 Timothy 3:12.)

8. Is danger necessarily a bad thing? Defend your answer.

9. How can we help those we love to be lifted up?

— ❧My Progress❧ —

What have you learned about safety being from the Lord?

11

Be Responsible When Fueling Fires

"Where there is no wood, the fire goes
out; and where there is no talebearer,
strife ceases." Proverbs 26:20

In order for any type of energy to be produced, there must
be some type of fuel—something that is consumed, something that is burned. A central heating unit can use natural gas
while a human body uses calories from food. The heart of man
may use positive sources of energy that affirm the goodness
that can be found in mortals, or mankind may employ negative methods of producing energy that deny a benevolent nature of humanity. All too frequently, I see evidence of the latter.
I am afraid that we hurt one another as much, if not more often, than we help.

We especially do great harm when we meddle in the affairs
of others and concern ourselves with matters that are none of
our business. Solomon remarked that when we interfere in situations we should not, we are like "one who takes a dog by
the ears" (Proverbs 26:17). That can be a dangerous thing to

do. The apostle Peter classified meddling or nosy interference along with what we call big sins: "But let none of you suffer as a murderer, a thief, an evildoer, or as a busybody in other people's matters" (1 Peter 4:15).

Words of Jest

Solomon also noted that if we intrude into the concerns of others, we are "like a madman who throws firebrands, arrows, and death," even if we do it lightheartedly and say, "I was only joking!" (Proverbs 26:18–19).

Remarks made in jest sometimes cut to the core of the spirit just as those said in anger or hostility. Sometimes kidding remarks about something that involves a sensitive area in our lives can hurt us more than a remark made out of cruelty, simply because the one who is displaying the inappropriate humor is quite often a friend. Most of us can remember the taunts of childhood friends: "Freckles," "Four Eyes," "Fatty," or "Beanpole." Though often said in jest and seemingly with affection, painful comments might remain with us all our lives. We need to be very careful concerning the remarks we make to and about each other.

Words of Criticism

We should be especially watchful in our criticism of one another. Quite often the critic is doing the devil's work rather than the Lord's. Those in positions of leadership in the church sometimes needlessly fall prey to unjust and undeserved criticism, simply because it is impossible to cater to everyone's desires or whims and at the same time please God and promote the cause of Christ.

A bulletin article by Dalton Key told of an incident on a train. Passengers were disturbed by the constant crying of a young child whom a father was trying to comfort. One person finally said, "Why don't you take that baby to its mother?" The young father's reply was, "This baby's mother is in the baggage car—in a casket." We need to make certain of our facts before we criticize.

Key went on to write,

> Quite often the critic is doing the devil's work rather than the Lord's.

Criticism requires no real talent. As someone has said, "Just a little thoughtlessness, mixed with a generous helping of self-centeredness, topped with a touch of self-righteousness, are about all the ingredients needed to bring pain and destroy a spirit." Before we criticize, we should ask ourselves some pointed questions:

- Is my criticism really necessary?
- Will I be helping or hurting the one criticized?
- What are my motives? Are they pure?
- Am I guilty of an equal or more serious offense myself?
- Am I aware of all the facts?

Let's think first; criticize later—if at all.

I say "Amen" to that.

➤ Words of Gossip

Here is another way to render the last portion of Proverbs 26:20: "So where there is no whisperer, the strife is silent." Gossip cannot be spread if we refuse to repeat it, or even better, if we decline to listen to it in the first place. Proverbs 16:28 reminds us that "a whisperer separates the best of friends."

In the July 1986 issue of the *Magnolia Messenger*, there was an unsigned poem that defines and exposes gossip for what it is.

Remember Me?

My name is Gossip.
I have no respect for justice.
I maim without killing.
I break hearts and ruin lives.
I am cunning and malicious
And gather strength with age.

The more I am quoted, the more I am believed.
I flourish at every level of society.
My victims are helpless.
They cannot protect themselves against me
Because I have no name and no face.

To track me down is impossible;
The harder you try, the more elusive I become.
I am nobody's friend.
Once I tarnish a reputation,
It is never quite the same.

I topple governments and wreck marriages.
I ruin careers, cause sleepless nights,
Heartaches, and indigestion.
I spawn suspicion and generate grief.

I make innocent people cry in their pillows.
Even my name hisses.
I am called Gossip.

I make headlines and headaches.
Before you repeat a story, ask yourself,
Is it true? Is it fair? Is it necessary?
If not, shut up!

I've never liked those two little words "shut up," but perhaps there is a time and place for them, or maybe we should simply say to ourselves and others, "Be quiet," when we are tempted to gossip about or disparage people.

Kind Words, Not Gossip

When I was a little girl, we had a manual water pump in our backyard. Before it would pump water, it had to be primed. We had to put water in to get water out.

We kept an old can nearby that always had a supply of water in it for use in priming the pump. Sometimes the water in that can would get muddy or dirty, so the first liquid that came out of the pump would be cloudy and murky also. It would take a good bit of pumping, physically moving the handle up and down, before the water would run clear. That is the way with our minds, if we fill them initially with gossip or bad thoughts.

Those things will come forth first. Prime your consciousness and your conscience with kind words and supportive expressions, and those things will be at the forefront of your existence. They will have prominence in your life. Don't prime the pump of conversation with gossip.

Fuels That Sustain

The first portion of the text for this chapter could also apply to some other areas in our lives. "Where there is no wood, the fire goes out" (Proverbs 26:20). In this instance, wood is the fuel that sustains the blaze. We can draw an analogy here to our spiritual lives. There are various types of fuel that can maintain and nourish the flame, the burning enthusiasm that should be a part of our relationship with God in order for Him to lift us up.

+ *Tribulation* can increase the glow of our spiritual existence. Pain or any kind of sorrow can make contact with God of the ultimate importance. If there are no challenges or discomfort in our lives, we may become complacent, and the fire will go out. A psalmist writes, "For You, O God, have tested us; You have refined us as silver is refined" (Psalm 66:10). Adversity can actually make us stronger spiritually as we lean on the Father and His blessed Son for comfort and strength. Having to deal with life's hazards and heartaches may very well serve to make us more committed to keeping the fire of Christianity blazing in our hearts.

+ *Prayer on a regular basis and with a sincere heart* will keep the flame from flickering. In fact, prayer is one of the best fuels that I know of to keep us close to God. Relationships fail when there is a lack of communication. Christians must talk to God to keep the spiritual fire burning.

✦ *Bible study* is essential in order to keep the fire blazing. Reading and meditating on Scripture and putting God's Word to work in our lives is of utmost importance. I did the math, and I learned that if I read and studied only five pages a day in my favorite Bible that I can read it through each year. Five pages is not very much material to both consider and understand. I am in my twentieth year of that experiment, and what a blessing it has been and what a help in keeping my spiritual fire aflame.

✦ *Fellowship and close interaction with other Christians* are sources of energy to keep the flame high. We need each other. That is one reason that the Lord created the special family known as the church, and it is perhaps a primary reason the inspired writer of Hebrews cautioned us about forsaking the assembly (Hebrews 10:25).

✦ *Attendance to formal worship services* will keep the blaze burning bright and high. Jesus promised to be with us when we assemble (Matthew 18:20). God will always be where His people gather together on a regular and dedicated basis. That is where we need to be. Paul acknowledged that it is through the church that we give glory to Jesus. "To Him be glory in the church by Christ Jesus to all generations, forever and ever. Amen" (Ephesians 3:21). We need to assemble with the other saints. It is in the church that we give glory to God.

Let us resolve to destroy from our lives any fuel that will cause the wrong kind of heat or produce energy for bad reasons. Let us replace that fuel with sources of power that will maintain our spiritual light and ensure that God will continue to lift us up.

— ⇒Questions⇐ —

1. Do we help one another more often than we hurt one another? Explain your answer.

2. What happens when we interfere, especially with the wrong motives, in the lives of others?

3. Should we use humor to insult or hurt someone? Why or why not?

4. Is criticism good or bad? Explain your answer.

5. Why does gossip cause strife? Have you ever been the victim of gossip?

6. List scriptures that demonstrate that gossiping is a sin.

7. What kinds of fuel should we have in our lives to keep our spirituality alight and alive?

8. Why is church attendance so important? (Read Hebrews 10:24–25.)

— ⇒ My Progress ⇐ —

What have you learned about gossip?

12

Dole Out the Honey

"Have you found honey? Eat only as
much as you need, lest you be filled
with it and vomit." Proverbs 25:16

Too much of a good thing can be just as bad as not
enough. Sufficiency or moderation should be our goal
rather than excess in every area of our lives, if we intend for
God to lift us up.

Less Can Be Best

When I was a little girl working in the fields, the first time each
season that we chopped cotton, we had to cut a lot of the stalks,
because the planter had dropped too many seeds. Thinning the
cotton was necessary to assure a good crop. My father showed
me how to select to cut down the weakest seedlings. The idea
was to leave the healthiest plants several inches apart so that
they would have nutrients and more room to grow. It was difficult for me to understand that having more cotton plants was
not better, but I followed my father's instructions. The ancient
Greek adage, "nothing in excess," applies to more than just
cotton fields.

William Shakespeare phrased that thought poetically in his drama, *King John*.

> To be possess'd with double pomp,
> To guard a title that was rich before,
> To gild refined gold, to paint the lily,
> To throw perfume on the violet,
> To smooth the ice, or add another hue
> Unto the rainbow, or with taper-light
> To seek the beauteous eye of heaven to garnish,
> Is wasteful and ridiculous excess.

Act IV, Scene ii

Too Much Knowledge

Even an excess of knowledge can be a hindrance. Ralph Waldo Emerson wrote, "The wise through excess of wisdom is made a fool." A better source that shows the hindrance of too much knowledge is the book of Ecclesiastes.

Solomon spoke from experience when he said,

> I communed with my heart, saying, "Look, I have attained greatness, and have gained more wisdom than all who have been before me in Jerusalem. My heart has understood great wisdom and knowledge." And I set my heart to know wisdom and to know madness and folly. I perceived that this also is grasping for the wind. For in much wisdom is much grief, and he who increases knowledge increases sorrow (Ecclesiastes 1:16–18).

Solomon's vast worldly knowledge could not prevent him from sinning when he followed after the idolatry of his many wives (Nehemiah 13:26). I truly hope that Solomon's wisdom concerning God was enough to make him return to the Lord. We are not really told about Solomon's last state of existence, but he certainly is another individual I would like to meet in heaven.

Isaiah prophesied concerning the wisdom of this world when he quoted the Lord:

> Therefore, behold, I will again do a marvelous work among this people, a marvelous work and a wonder; for the wisdom of their wise men shall perish, and the understanding of their prudent men shall be hidden (Isaiah 29:14).

Paul wrote about the fulfillment of that same prophecy.

> For it is written: "I will destroy the wisdom of the wise, and bring to nothing the understanding of the prudent." Where is the wise? Where is the scribe? Where is the disputer of this age? Has not God made foolish the wisdom of this world? For since, in the wisdom of God, the world through wisdom did not know God, it pleased God through the foolishness of the message preached to save those who believe (1 Corinthians 1:19–21).

We need to be wary of obtaining too much of the wrong kind of knowledge or education that will lead us to think we do not need God any longer. Please don't misinterpret my thoughts; I most certainly value education. I was the first in a family of nine children to graduate from high school and the only one of nine to receive a college diploma. I went on to do graduate work above the master's level. Yet all too often, secular education can fill us with an overwhelming pride in self and imbue us with a harmful, materialistic independence that can curtail spiritual growth. An excess of learning that causes us to feel so intelligent and sophisticated that we think it is acceptable to change the Word that He has left for us will certainly lead to our downfall.

Sometimes we may develop what passes for intelligence to such a degree that the obvious escapes us. It was Jesus Himself who said,

> I thank You, Father, Lord of heaven and earth, that You have hidden these things from the wise and prudent and revealed them to babes. Even so, Father, for so it seemed good in Your sight (Luke 10:21).

Our hearts and our minds should be open to all that God's Word has to teach us.

Avoid Foolish Disputes

Of course, I suppose it is even possible to have too much knowledge of the Scriptures if we do not have the good sense to use that knowledge in the right manner—if we quibble over inconsequential details. Paul advised Titus, "But avoid foolish disputes, genealogies, contentions, and strivings about the law; for they are unprofitable and useless" (Titus 3:9). The advice Paul gave Timothy was almost identical. "But avoid foolish and ignorant disputes, knowing that they generate strife" (2 Timothy 2:23).

I have so many unanswered questions that come to mind as I study the Holy Scriptures day by day. Yet I hope I will always realize that the Word of God is sufficient and complete as it stands. The New Testament plan of salvation and the way to heaven are laid out clearly. I should possess enough wisdom to read the Bible and follow its precepts which will make me pleasing to the Father and lead me to an eternal home with Him. I also need to have enough comprehension and familiarity with God's Word that I am able to teach others the gospel. In addition, I must have adequate knowledge in order to have the ability to defend my faith (Philippians 1:17; 1 Peter 3:15). Anything else that I wish to know can be discovered when I meet God and our blessed Savior face to face, if by that time my questions still seem important enough to ask.

Neither Poverty nor Riches

The concept of too much honey can also invade our view of money. An excess of material wealth can cause problems for us. A friend told me once that she had never heard me wish for things or complain about not having something. Well,

> Why not provide powdered milk to an orphanage rather than buy the latest fashion trend?

I don't think she has always listened too closely to me. However, I don't concentrate on things more than I do on people. Perhaps it comes from being poor as a child, but I have never been concerned with possessing a lot of money, possibly because it seemed so out of reach. Like most women, I do like nice things, but if there is food on the table and clothes on my back, I refuse to complain. It is difficult for me to understand the thinking of those who are obsessed with certain designers or labels. Why not provide powdered milk to an orphanage rather than buy the latest fashion trend?

Now don't misunderstand me. I believe in making preparation for rainy days and old age. God has blessed my husband and me financially so much more than I ever expected or deserved. Still, this business of seeing how much money can be made and accumulated just for the sake of having it seems meaningless unless perhaps one agrees with Andrew Carnegie who once said, "Surplus wealth is a sacred trust which its possessor is bound to administer in his lifetime for the good of the community."

A sensible request is made in Proverbs 30. Agur proclaimed,

Give me neither poverty nor riches—feed me with the food allotted to me; lest I be full, and deny You, and say, "Who is the Lord?" Or lest I be poor and steal, and profane the name of my God (Proverbs 30:8–9).

Beware of Abundance

Studies have shown that the happiest people are those who are not very rich or very poor. It is the extremes that cause problems. Being middle class, economically speaking, may not be very exciting, but it tends to produce better-adjusted individuals. There is a feeling of satisfaction in working for what one has and in planning how to use what one earns. Life could eventually become very boring or even meaningless if we were in a position to get everything we wanted without any effort on our part, though I admit it might seem enjoyable for a little while.

The apostle Paul gave Timothy some good advice concerning wealth. We would do well to take note of it also. Paul wrote,

> Now godliness with contentment is great gain. For we brought nothing into this world, and it is certain we can carry nothing out. And having food and clothing, with these we shall be content (1 Timothy 6:6–8).

We should remember that Paul was inspired of God when he wrote those words, and that what he said has application for us today. Jesus Christ had no real estate investments, certificates of deposit, or even a retirement plan. That is not to imply that those things are wrong. We just need to be careful that they do not control us. Remember Proverbs 25:16 concerning honey? With money, especially an unhealthy obsession with it, as

Give me neither poverty nor riches.

—Proverbs 30:8

with honey, we don't want to be "filled with it and vomit." Solomon said, "The abundance of the rich will not permit him to sleep" (Ecclesiastes 5:12). A profusion of worldly possessions will not be the reason God lifts us up. In fact, those assets could be the reason we fall from grace, if we place too much value on obtaining and keeping those things. We need to remember the rich fool who lost it all (Luke 12:16–21). Jesus Himself said, "Take heed and beware of covetousness, for one's life does not consist in the abundance of the things which he possesses" (Luke 12:15).

If we truly want God to lift us up, we will practice moderation in all things. When we find honey, we will partake of it sparingly.

— ❧Questions❧ —

1. Why should moderation be a goal of the Christian?

2. Can one have too much knowledge? Explain your answer.

3. Explain Ecclesiastes 1:16–18.

4. Did Solomon always apply his great wisdom to his own life? How do you know?

5. What has God "revealed unto babes"? (Read Luke 10:21.)

6. Explain the warning in Titus 3:9.

7. How can having too little or too much wealth be a problem? (Read Proverbs 30:8–9.)

8. What advice did Paul give Timothy concerning contentment? Is it possible to be content without godliness?

9. According to Jesus, of what should not be the primary focus of our lives? (Read Luke 12:15.)

10. Is it possible that wealth could cause us to fall from grace? Support your answer with scriptures.

— ❧My Progress❧ —

What have you learned about excess?

13

Seek to Be Well-Advised

"By pride comes nothing but strife, but with the well-advised is wisdom." Proverbs 13:10

English psychologist and writer Havelock Ellis once wrote, "The Promised Land always lies on the other side of a wilderness." I believe that is a legitimate thought. Nothing of real value can be ours without effort on our part, and perhaps pain or even despair may be involved at some point along the way as we strive to achieve goals. In this life, there will always be wildernesses through which the Christian must travel, and often as soon as we conquer one, another wasteland will be in sight.

The children of Israel wandered in the wilderness of the peninsula of Sinai for forty years before coming to their promised land. Those individuals had much to learn during their wanderings—such concepts as trust, obedience, and patience. God had rescued the Hebrews from Egypt, but so many of them would die in the wilderness because they lacked the wisdom to listen to Him and obey. Only two of the adults over age twenty proved themselves capable of learning to trust and obey God in order to leave the wilderness behind. Joshua and Caleb were remarkable individuals indeed.

➤ Navigating the Wilderness

✦ *Trust.* God expects us to trust Him. He has never failed to take care of His own. When destruction seemed imminent, God fed, cared for, and protected the Israelites. Still the Hebrew people could not seem to see beyond the wilderness. Several generations later David would write, "I have been young, and now am old; yet I have not seen the righteous forsaken, nor his descendants begging bread" (Psalm 37:25). It was David's son Solomon who would remind us, "Trust in the Lord with all your heart, and lean not on your own understanding; in all your ways acknowledge Him, and He shall direct your paths" (Proverbs 3:5–6). I am told that the word *direct* in that passage actually means to make smooth or straight. What a wonderful thought that when we trust in God, He will remove obstacles from our paths!

✦ *Obedience.* For whatever reason, the children of Israel would not allow themselves to learn that God expects obedience—complete obedience even though the matter might seem trivial. I'm reminded of the man who gathered sticks on the Sabbath, thus breaking one of God's laws. The Lord was explicit when He told the people to stone that man to death (Numbers 15:32–36). Saul, the first king of Israel, had difficulty grasping the need for obedience. It was Samuel, who was both prophet and priest, who reminded Saul, "Has the Lord as great delight in burnt offerings and sacrifices, as in obeying the voice of the Lord? Behold, to obey is better than sacrifice, and to heed than the fat of rams" (1 Samuel 15:22).

Of course, now we have a much better covenant than that of the Old Testament; yet if we are to make it beyond the wilderness of this world, we must still obey God. The good news of Christ is a better way, but that gospel also contains some exact instructions for us to follow. Sometimes we allow our pride to get in the way of accepting that truth of the better way, which is in Jesus Christ, and we are not well-advised. Our punishment for disobedience is not always immediate as in the stoning of the man who gathered sticks, but we will certainly be accountable to God (2 Corinthians 5:10).

✦ *Patience.* It always amazes me when I stop to think that even after witnessing so many miracles, the Israelites remained so anxious and impatient. God's people have to endure. Patience is one of those virtues that we are to develop (James 1:2–4). We must be willing to wait. If I am honest with myself, however, I wonder if I would have been any different had I been numbered among those who wandered the wilderness of Sinai.

Pride Breeds Strife

If we are not careful, the quality that will keep us in the wilderness, isolated from God, is the emotion pride, which was mentioned earlier. There is another passage in Proverbs that deals with this harmful characteristic.

Pride goes before destruction, and a haughty spirit before a fall. Better to be of a humble spirit with the lowly, than to divide the spoil with the proud. He who heeds the word wisely will find good, and whoever trusts in the Lord, happy is he (Proverbs 16:18–20).

Pride breeds spiritual blindness and gives birth to a sense of false security. Pride prevents us from trusting God. In fact, pride will keep us from God, and we will not be set on high.

David, the shepherd boy, warrior, and king, knew this. "Though the Lord is on high, yet He regards the lowly; but the proud He knows from afar" (Psalm 138:6). I don't know about you, but I don't want to be "far off" from God. I want the Father to be up close and personal in my life.

Solomon proclaimed that pride causes contention, but this son of David also tells us as he personifies wisdom, "The fear of the Lord is to hate evil; pride and arrogance and the evil way and the perverse mouth I hate" (Proverbs 8:13). If a child of God is well-advised, he will not be overly proud or possess a spirit of arrogance.

> "I will bring you down from there," says the Lord.
>
> —Jeremiah 49:16

We need to be careful that our pride or an overdeveloped sense of self-sufficiency does not encourage us to attempt to lift ourselves up. Only God can do that.

Do you remember when the Lord had Jeremiah speak to the Edomites? "Against Edom. Thus says the Lord of hosts: 'Is wisdom no more in Teman? Has counsel perished from the prudent? Has their wisdom vanished?'" (Jeremiah 49:7). These people were not well-advised. They looked to themselves and their idols rather than to the living God, and they suffered greatly for their behavior.

Jeremiah went on to admonish them for their attitude.

> "Your fierceness has deceived you, the pride of your heart, O you who dwell in the clefts of the rock, who hold the height of the hill! Though you make your nest as high as the eagle, I will bring you down from there," says the Lord (Jeremiah 49:16).

Sooner or later, God will humble all those who do not look to Him to be lifted up, and He will destroy the independence, power, and pride of those who think they don't need Him.

Let God Lift You Up

No matter what wilderness we face—whether it be sickness, financial problems, loss of loved ones, betrayal by friends or family, disobedient children, perhaps even the bitterness of our own hearts (Proverbs 14:10) or just difficulties with life in general—God can lead us out to the promised land if we trust, if we obey, and if we wait. When we are willing to do those things, we are well-advised and we have gained wisdom. We can be assured that God will then lift us up.

According to Ralph Waldo Emerson, "The wise man in the storm prays to God, not for safety from danger, but for deliverance from fear. It is the storm within which endangers him, not the storm without." One of my favorite Bible verses reminds me that God is not the origin of any fear that might lie within me: "For God has not given a spirit of fear, but of power and of love and of a sound mind" (2 Timothy 1:7).

Press on Despite Danger

Fear cripples and destroys, and it must be overcome if we are to experience happiness. Our fears may have as their base very real difficulties that we must strive to conquer, but if we are not very diligent, the overwhelming, anxious worry created by our fears may keep us from being victorious. Mark Rutherford put it another way. "When we are afraid, we ought not to occupy ourselves with endeavoring to prove that there is no danger, but in strengthening ourselves to go on in spite of the danger." Fear, whether seemingly justified or not, should never be allowed to put our lives on hold. Fear should not control us.

Fear keeps us from being well-advised because it makes problems seem worse than they are. Anxious worry can prevent us from dealing adequately with difficulties life may send our way. The apostle Paul gave the church at Philippi good advice for dealing with fear, and it is still applicable for us today:

> Rejoice in the Lord always. Again I will say, rejoice! Let your gentleness be known to all men. The Lord *is* at hand. Be anxious for nothing, but in everything by prayer and supplication, with thanksgiving, let your requests be made known to God; and the peace of God, which surpasses all understanding, will guard your hearts and minds through Christ Jesus (Philippians 4:4–7).

Then, too, hope is an antidote for fear. When my husband Bob was diagnosed with acute leukemia, his attending physician, Dr. Steven Wolfe of Vander-bilt Medical Center, said, "Come to Nash-ville; things may not be as bad as you think." Precious hope, offered in kind-ness and acted upon in joy, can accom-plish wonders.

> *Be anxious for nothing.*
> —**Philippians 4:6**

It is true that acute leukemia eventu-ally triumphed over Bob's body, but it did not conquer his spirit. Instead of a mere two weeks, he was given eighteen more pre-cious months. Hope made Bob a brave warrior. Even though we may not always surmount troubles in this world, God will lift His children up in the next one every time. Trust in God made Bob the ultimate victor.

Sometimes we worry needlessly. I have always been a great one for borrowing trouble, but I am striving to do better. Some-one observed that if ten troubles are coming down the road, nine will run into the ditch before they get to us. Some of us, on the other hand, jump into the middle of the road and say, "Hit me; hit me!" If that won't do it, sometimes we actually jump into the ditch with the troubles. Too many of us seem de-termined to find something to fear.

We would be well-advised not to be afraid to be happy, even if that happiness might be taken away from us somewhere down the line. God is going to lift up those who belong to Him and set them on high. We just need to give Him time to do it.

— ⚜Questions⚜ —

1. What are some of the things we should learn as we wander through the wildernesses of this current world?

2. How do you know that God expects obedience in all things? (Read 1 Samuel 15:22.)

3. What sinful quality will keep us in the wilderness and prevent God from lifting us up? Explain your answer.

4. What lesson can we learn from the Edomites?

5. Does everyone face a wilderness of some sort? If so, what is yours?

6. What will fear do to us? What are some biblical models for dealing with fear?

7. Do most of us worry needlessly? (Read Philippians 4:6–7.)

8. Whom will God lift up at some point in time? How do you know this?

— ⚜My Progress⚜ —

What have you learned about being certain that you are well-advised?

Addendum

The process of allowing God to lift us up is continuous, and it extends from the present to the future when the Father is the center of our existence. Because He made us creatures of choice, God will not force Himself on us. We have to be willing participants in this journey in which He lifts us up above the fray which is this life on earth.

The prophet Micah understood our responsibility to God when he wrote, "He has shown you, O man, what is good; and what does the Lord require of you but to do justly, to love mercy, and to walk humbly with your God?" (Micah 6:8).

When we are striving to walk in the light (1 John 1:7), when we love the Father, when we imitate the Son and keep His commandments (John 15:14), when we allow His Spirit to dwell in us (Acts 5:32), our future is secure.

The psalmist wrote,

> Because he has set his love upon Me, therefore, I
>   will deliver him;
> I will set him on high, because he has known My
>   name.
> He shall call upon Me, and I will answer him;
> I will be with him in trouble;
> I will deliver him and honor him.
>
> Psalm 91:14–15

How wonderful is that?

Sources Cited

Golding, William. *Lord of the Flies* (New York, N.Y.: Penguin, 1954).

Fitzsimons, Tim. "A Record 4.5 Percent of U.S. Adults Identify as LGBT, Gallup Estimates." NBC News.com. May 25, 2018. https://www.nbc news.com/feature/nbc-out/record-4-5-percent-u-s-adults-identify-lgbt -gallup-n877486.

Innes, Michael. *The Bloody Wood* (Cornwall: Stratus Books, 1966).

Newman, John Henry. "Sermon 20: Wisdom and Innocence" (ca. 1843-1869), NewmanReader.org. Accessed April 23, 2019. http://www .newmanreader.org/works/subjects/sermon20.html.

Thoreau, Henry David. *The Writings of Henry David Thoreau, Journal 1850. September 15, 1851,* Bradford Torrey, ed. (Cambridge: Riverside Press, 1906).

CPSIA information can be obtained
at www.ICGtesting.com
Printed in the USA
FFHW020854130519
52388529-57811FF